MANTIS
BOXING ANTHOLOGY

An Anthology of Articles from the
Journal of Asian Martial Arts

Compiled by Michael A. DeMarco, M.A.

Disclaimer
Please note that the authors and publisher of this book are not responsible in any manner whatsoever for any injury that may result from practicing the techniques and/or following the instructions given within. Since the physical activities described herein may be too strenuous in nature for some readers to engage in safely, it is essential that a physician be consulted prior to training.

All Rights Reserved
No part of this publication, including illustrations, may be reproduced or utilized in any form or by any means, electronic or mechanical, including photocopying, recording, or by any information storage and retrieval system (beyond that copying permitted by sections 107 and 108 of the US Copyright Law and except by reviewers for the public press), without written permission from Via Media Publishing Company.

Warning: Any unauthorized act in relation to a copyright work may result in both a civil claim for damages and criminal prosecution.

Copyright © 2016
by Via Media Publishing Company
941 Calle Mejia #822, Santa Fe, NM 87501 USA

All articles in this anthology were originally
published in the *Journal of Asian Martial Arts*, and
Asian Martial Arts: Constructive Thoughts & Practical Application.
Listed according to the table of contents for this anthology:

Eisen, M. (1993), Vol. 2 No. 1, pp. 70-83
Amos, D. (1997), Vol. 6 No 4, pp. 30-61
Edwards, D. (2000), Vol. 9 No. 3, pp. 86-97
Profatilov, I. (2001), Vol. 10 No. 4, pp. 44-75
Profatilov, I. (2012), In *Asian Martial Arts: Constructive Thoughts & Practical Applications*, pp. 114-117

Book and cover design by
Via Media Publishing Company

Edited by
Michael A. DeMarco, M.A.

Cover illustration
© Cover Illustration by Joukinthesky.com

ISBN: 9781983765375

www.viamediapublishing.com

contents

iv **Preface**
by Michael DeMarco, M.A.

CHAPTERS

1 **Gin-foon Mark: Classical Versus Modern Gongfu**
by Martin Eisen, Ph.D.

13 **A Hong Kong Southern Praying Mantis Cult**
by Daniel M. Amos, Ph.D.

43 **Character Formulas in Seven Star Praying Mantis**
by Dwight C. Edwards

55 **The Traditional History of Plum Blossom Praying Mantis Boxing**
by Ilya Profatilov, M.A.

95 **Taiji Da: A Mantis Boxing Close-Range Technique**
by Ilya Profatilov, M.A.

99 **Index**

preface

A praying mantis insect faces any danger regardless of it's opponent's size and strength. If you've seen their parade of innate fearlessness, it is easy to see why they have inspired the creation of a Chinese martial art style. This anthology assembles the work of four highly qualified authors who present rare information about praying mantis boxing.

In the first chapter, Dr. Martin Eisen interviews Gin-foon Mark, a noted fifth-generation master of Guangxi Province Bamboo Grove Praying Mantis. Mark discusses training in Chinese temples and compares it with the common training methods found today. The goals, training, and results are very different. The classical methods include developing the senses for fighting, and medical applications.

Dr. Daniel Amos studied praying mantis boxing in Hong Kong. When a person starts to study a martial art, he or she is actually joining a social group to do so. The social structures of Hong Kong martial arts temple cults provide Chinese shunted aside by the dominant status system with an alternative, albeit secondary, system of status achievement. Here, the author presents details of his study and the social setting.

The essence of China's varied martial styles has often been preserved in writings. At the heart of this heritage are "character formulas": a short list of characters that is used to establish the most elemental characteristics of a particular martial style. In the third chapter, Dwight Edwards provides an analysis of "The Twelve Character Formula of Seven Star Praying Mantis Boxing."

In the following chapter, Ilya Profatilov shares the results of years of researching the mantis systems in China. Old manuscripts describe the origins, theory, and curriculum of praying mantis boxing. Additionally, oral folk traditions, legends, fantastic stories, and songs are utlized. Referencing such sources, the author details the history of this realistic combat system, showing that it preserves its original techniques and classical forms. In the final chapter Profatilov discusses a favored close-range technique he recounts from his tutalage under Master Lin Tangfang (1920-2009) in a small village in Shandong Province. He uses the past to inspire his practice, as we hope this anthology will stimulate further research and practice to all readers.

> Michael A. DeMarco, Publisher
> Santa Fe, New Mexico
> October 2016

chapter 1

Gin-foon Mark: Classical Versus Modern Gongfu
by Martin Eisen, Ph.D.

Gin-foon Mark with double-butterfly knives.
Photograph courtesy of Gin-foon Mark.

Background

Born near Guangzhou city on September 14, 1927, Gin-foon Mark embodies a long tradition of Chinese cultural studies with a special devotion to martial arts. Today, he is the fifth-generation master of a style known in Cantonese as *Kwong Sai Jook Lum* (in Mandarin as *Guangxi Zhu Lin*, Guangxi Province's Bamboo Grove) Praying Mantis. Coming from a direct family lineage of high ranking gongfu experts, his own instruction in gongfu began at the age of five under the supervision of his uncles and grandfather. At age nine he was admitted to the Shaolin Temple at Song Mountain where he received training in Shaolin, White Crane, Eagle Claw, Leopard and Tiger styles. He also studied Tiger Claw in Macao's Hoi Jung Temple and praying mantis in the Jook Lum Monastery in Guandong Province. In these monasteries, Gin-foon Mark was schooled in *ming-gong* (self-defense and healing arts); *shen-gong* (spirit gongfu); *qigong* (the use of internal power for martial arts and health). He continued his studies of praying mantis in the United States under Wing-fai Lum for ten more years. Just before Mr. Lum retired and moved to Taiwan, he designated Mark to be his successor in accordance with established traditions.

Government officials of Minnesota, Mark's home state, consider him such a noteworthy figure that he was elected to their Living History Museum. Mark is one of the few living people who studied in the monasteries when they were still cultural centers and strongholds of gongfu. He has been teaching gongfu in the United States for about forty-five years and visits China frequently. Thus, he is an ideal person to compare classical gongfu with modern gongfu in the United States and China. The differences in goals and training between modern and classical gongfu will be apparent from the following interview.

INTERVIEW

Q: What was gongfu training like in the monasteries?

GFM: You had to have patience. In the beginning martial arts were never mentioned. First, we trained all the senses. Long periods of meditation preceded and followed each training period. We were blindfolded for all the sensory exercises. We had to distinguish herbs, incense, animals and other material by smell.

Q: I suppose the martial arts application was to detect a hidden enemy by smell. Were there any other applications?

GFM: Monks could tell some of the ingredients in an herbal mixture by smelling it. There were no devices for telling time in many chambers in the temple. Different smelling incense sticks were lit each hour to tell the time.

Q: What were some of the hearing exercises?

GFM: We were blindfolded and sat in the center of a circle of monks. When a monk made a noise, we had to tell which direction it came from. A similar exercise was to tell the direction and the distance of an object from the noise it made when dropped. We had to try and hear a grain of rice thrown in the air. A stick or sword was struck and we had to tell whether it was hit at the top, middle or bottom.

Q: The obvious martial art applications of these last exercises is to detect a surprise or rear attack by hearing. Could you mention some other applications?

GFM: You can tell which part of the foe's sword you contact by the sound. The hearing exercises were very helpful for avoiding bullets and shells while fighting in the Sino-Japanese War. Enemies could be detected in the dark.

Q: Although smelling and hearing training are useful, I don't think they can account for your outstanding hand techniques. Did you practice any sort of yielding or sensitivity exercises?

GFM: Yes. We began by sitting in a chair opposite our partner. We were blindfolded. A simple beginning exercise was to hold your hand, palm up, in front of your body. Your partner would gently push down on your palm. You would try to move your hand in the direction of the force and turn it over, so that your palm was face down. Your opponent would now push up and you would try to move your hand upward and rotate it so that your palm faced up.

Q: I suppose that this exercise was designed to teach you to relax, offer no resistance and move in the direction of your opponent's force.

GFM: Correct. After becoming proficient in the one-hand exercise both hands were used. Your partner could push either hand or both simultaneously. When both hands were pushed, each hand could be pushed in a different direction. After a while the hands could be pushed in any direction, not just vertically. Similar exercises were done for the legs. Later, other parts of the body were pushed.

Q: Were these exercises only practiced sitting down?

GFM: No. They were practiced sitting down initially so that you could relax more and not become tense because of a poor stance. After you became proficient in the sitting exercises, they were practiced standing still. Later, they were practiced moving and other exercises were added. For example, we would bump into each other and practice neutralizing and using the opponent's force against him. Our feet were tied together and we had to move in unison in various ways by using only feeling, since we were still blindfolded.

Q: Were practical applications of these sensitivity exercises discussed in this stage of your training?

GFM: Applications were not discussed until you became proficient in the sensory exercises. In general nothing was explained. Explanations are the American way or the modern way in China. You were shown an exercise and told to practice it thousands of times. You would not be shown another technique until you mastered the previous one. You might finally understand a technique through your practice. Verbal explanations were not given.

Q: Did you practice self-defense after mastering the sensory exercises?

GFM: Even after passing through the sensitivity part of your training, you didn't learn to punch, kick or block. You had to practice exercises designed to loosen and relax every part of your body. You had to practice footwork and stances for a long time. Many hours were devoted to qigong and meditation exercises. You had to develop a great deal of power in single techniques before you were allowed to practice combination techniques.

Q: Did you study weapons?
GFM: Yes, we studied all the classical weapons, but only after mastering all the unarmed techniques. Nowadays, students learn weapons right away. How can someone with no power, a poor stance and footwork, use a weapon? Even many instructors look like they're performing a juggling act during a weapons demonstration. They swing their weapons in large arcs; they don't have short power.

 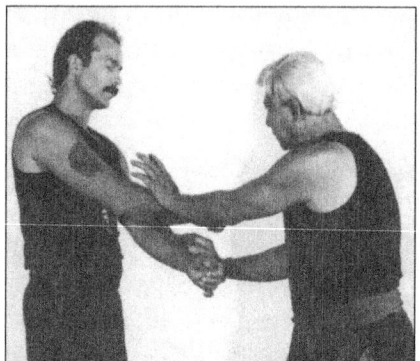

Left: Gin-foon Mark first blocks a left punch with his left forearm. Then he grabs his opponent's left wrist. Mark completes this sequence by attacking the elbow joint with his right forearm. A special thanks to Mark's student, Michael Flaherty, who is shown participating in some of these photos.

Right: As an attacker punches with his left hand, Mark slips his right hand downward, directing and controlling the left arm. The opponent follows with a right punch which is blocked crosswards, causing the opponent's right arm to press down onto his left arm, in effect pinning them together.

Q: Your system of praying mantis is famous for short power. How did you develop short power with weapons?
GFM: The only secret is patience and constant practice. I had to be very skilled and strong in unarmed techniques before I was allowed to practice weapons. My instructors made me practice single techniques, as cutting

potatoes, melons, etc., for six years before learning any forms.

Q: Your techniques are so powerful. Nowadays many students come to train once a week. In six years or in many situations much sooner, they think they are masters and open their own club. People don't seem to use common sense when thinking about martial arts. No one would think that a Ph.D. in physics, for example, could be obtained by attending a university once a week for an hour or two for six years.

GFM: I think that most of the old masters were more skillful than most modern masters. It is not because secret techniques were lost. Modern times are not conducive to learning gongfu. Many people have a lot of responsibilities such as their jobs, families, etc., and there are many different forms of amusement to distract people. When I was a boy, there were no radios, televisions, movies or books in our village. People did not have a lot of responsibilities or a demanding job. Consequently, I could practice nearly the whole day. Besides, training was one of the few forms of amusement.

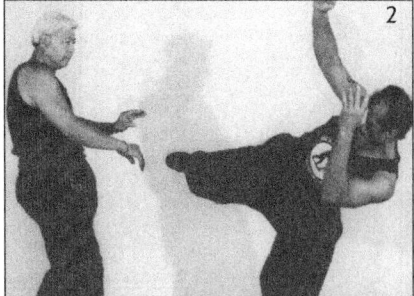

1): Mark traps both of the opponent's arms with his left hand and executes a right palm strike directly to the jaw.
2-3): M. Flaherty advances with a powerful kick from the right Gin-foon Mark steps left, catching the kick with a cross-block.

Mark encourages learning the intricacies of hand and leg movements through observation and long hours of practice.

Q: Did you only study self-defense in the monasteries?
GFM: No. The monks realized that it could be dangerous to only practice the yang part of gongfu (self-defense), without practicing the remaining yin part (meditation, Chinese medicine, art, etc.). They wanted to produce a well-rounded human being, not a killing machine. Since the monasteries were isolated, it was important to know medicine to treat sick people as well as injuries occurring during gongfu practice.

Q: I can attest to the fact that constant yang-type training often leads to a hard mind.
GFM: The students in monasteries were much better than most students in

modern, commercial gongfu schools. Monastic students had to have good character and aptitude to be admitted to the monastery. They couldn't pay to learn techniques and only learned new techniques when they had mastered the previous techniques to the satisfaction of the master. They had to have lots of patience and perseverance and were forced to train hard. Students were instilled with the love of learning. They realized that gongfu was a lifetime pursuit, since they saw that the masters were still studying. They were not given a false sense of pride in their accomplishments, since there were no rankings, in the modern sense.

Q: You mean that there were no colored belts or sashes. Was there more than one master for a system?

GFM: The students were classified as student or disciple. You didn't need a belt to know if you could do a technique. Wrestlers don't get belts. There was only one known master of a system. The other people trained because they liked it. When the master retired he appointed a successor. The existence of another master was kept secret. No one ever saw him train. He never taught any students. The reason for this secrecy was that, if the known master was killed, then the system would not perish, since the other master could take over.

Q: Did you study more than one style of gongfu in the monastery?

GFM: No. In fact, the style of gongfu was not mentioned. Learning one style takes a lifetime. Nowadays you often see commercial schools run by a teacher in his twenties purporting to teach a half dozen different styles. Many modern students want to learn a lot of styles. They remind me of the boy who wanted to fatten his cow. He took the cow up one mountain which had a green pasture. No sooner had he got there, he noticed what seemed to be a greener pasture on another mountain. So he dragged the cow up the other mountain. After remaining there a short time, he spotted what looked like a more lush pasture on another mountain. He dragged the cow to this new pasture. After repeating this process for awhile, he noticed that his cow had become skinnier.

Q: Do you think some styles might have some techniques not contained in other styles and so it might be advantageous to study them?

GFM: In the old days most styles were oriented to self-defense. The end result of their training was the same. The good fighters looked very similar when they fought. If modern students who are interested in self-defense could have seen these old masters, they might change their minds about learning different styles.

Gin-foon Mark, in a praying mantis posture, poses with the drum and lion costume used for special festivities. He has performed the lion dance in New York City for the Chinese New Year as part of his enthusiasm for sharing his Asian heritage.

Q: How did the old masters train their students to fight?
GFM: Real fighting is continuous. You attack, your opponent counters, you counter his counter and so on. The advanced students were taught realistic, two-men fighting formulas emphasizing the continuity of real fighting. Thus, students could practice and learn timing, distancing, feeling, using the opponent's strength against him, etc. These types of training exercises can no longer be found in most modern versions of these old systems. I have devised such two-person formulas for each one-person formula in my system.

Q: Where did you study the sensitivity exercises you described?
GFM: In the Hoi Jung Temple in Macao.

Q: Did you study praying mantis there?

GFM: No. I studied a version of tiger claw. It doesn't resemble most modern versions of tiger claw that I have seen. I applied these ideas to praying mantis. That is why my hand movements are softer than my instructors.

Q: **Why doesn't modern tiger claw resemble the system you were taught?**
GFM: Perhaps this system was lost. Modern masters are not solely motivated by practicality in fighting. They like to pose and flex their muscles. Many of them have not really studied the animals they are trying to imitate. The monks kept many animals in the monastery.

Q: **Did they keep the animals to learn their actions for fighting or qigong exercises?**
GFM: There were other reasons. Some were kept as pets. Others were trained to do useful tasks. Bears were trained to fetch water. We also fought the bears. This was good practice. The students became stronger from this training, but even the strongest student was not stronger than the bear. Thus, you had to learn proper timing and the correct angle of deflection to deflect the bear's cuff.

Q: **What led to the decline of gongfu in China?**
GFM: When the Communists came to power they tried to suppress gongfu, since it could be used against them. They persecuted masters, especially those who were good fighters. For example, my uncle was a famous gongfu expert. When the Red soldiers came to his village, they tried to force my uncle to kneel. This was humiliating and insulting, since only criminals knelt in China. The villagers begged my uncle to kneel. However, he refused saying that everyone must die sometime. My uncle had great inner power. The soldier shot him more than twenty times before he died. The masters who were not killed or imprisoned fled to Taiwan or went into hiding. The Communists thought that any form of religion was superstition. Monks were also persecuted and monasteries were closed.

Q: **In recent years the Chinese government has been encouraging the development of wushu. Do you think that this will revitalize gongfu in China?**
GFM: Wushu is designed to please spectators and judges. It consists of many large, exaggerated and acrobatic movements. The formulas are supposed to be based on classical formulas. However, the competitors are marked on originality and choreography. Thus, the old formulas are not preserved. Besides, I have never met any old masters of any classical system who knew that whole system on my trips to China. Therefore, instead of

preserving classical gongfu, encouraging the development of wushu will further weaken classical gongfu.

Q: Have you met a lot of people who were good fighters on your trips?

GFM: Some of the wushu people, especially the younger, athletic ones, thought they could fight. However, they were mediocre in comparison to the old, classically trained fighters. The practical applications of gongfu are still discouraged in China.

Q: Did you see any monasteries that were functioning as in olden times?

GFM: No. The government has reopened some monasteries as tourist attractions. They are filled with actors, not priests.

Q: Do you think that there are any masters, in the classical sense, left anywhere in the world? By this I mean a person who knows his complete system and was appointed the sole successor of the system by the previous master.

GFM: Very few. Even when I was a boy many of the older systems were incomplete. The masters had died before passing on the whole system. Although some had retained the forms, the practical applications were often lost. Fortunately, there have only been four previous masters in our system and none died before passing on the complete system.

Q: Do you think it is possible to bring gongfu to the level it was when you were a small boy in China?

GFM: It would be very difficult. There are very few masters alive today that know a complete style of gongfu. Students are not discriminating and don't seek out these people.

Q: Yes, it is very strange but parents of students don't investigate martial schools. However, if they were going to attend a university, they would investigate the schools thoroughly.

GFM: Times and attitudes are also different. As I mentioned previously, people don't have as much time for practicing. In the old days more people understood the virtues of hard work, respect of the ancient masters, humility, loyalty and respect of the teacher and his guidance.

Q: Similar difficulties are encountered in the education system in the USA. Many students don't respect their teachers, what instant enlightenment and rarely do their homework. What do you think about tournaments?

GFM: Generally, they are detrimental to gongfu. Many judges are not expert in the style they are judging. Competitors don't do a classical form but a choreographed, shortened version. They are frequently judged on how flashy their form looks and how well they can act and not how closely their form resembles the original or on practicality or power.

Grandmaster Wing-fai Lum and his five disciples in 1968.
Front row, l. to r.: Gin-foon Mark, Wing-fai Lum (Sung Lu), and Ho-dun Chin (died 1991). Back row, l. to r.: Bao Lee, Chuck Chin, and Show Ng. In the above listing, the family names follow given names.

Q: What about the other aspects of gongfu which were taught in the monasteries?

GFM: There are very few teachers who have studied the treatment of injuries or qigong for health. In the old days, the monasteries were isolated and medical help was not readily available. Thus, it was necessary to keep yourself healthy and to be able to treat illnesses.

Q: Today many students think that western medicine is sufficient. They regard Chinese medicine and qigong's unscientific and so don't want to devote time to study these arts. There is a lot of empirical evidence that these methods work and there are already some scientific investigations explaining some aspects of Chinese medicine.

GFM: Some of the ancient masters could perform amazing feats when they were aged. My Six Healing Sounds teacher was known as "Old Man" in China. At age ninety-eight, he looked half his age. Until his death, at about one hundred and five, he was very active and in excellent physical condition. He continued working for the government and travelled from province to province teaching qigong. Lee Siem, the second master of our system, was running around China building temples when he was over one hundred years old.

Q: Today most commercial gongfu schools don't teach Chinese painting or lion dancing.

GFM: In spite of the limited time of many students, I still try to teach these subjects and other arts taught in the monasteries.

Q: We are fortunate to have a complete, classical system today. All that is needed to preserve and spread it are dedicated students who are willing to spend a lifetime studying and improving this system.

GFM: Yes. However, one can learn to improve and preserve one's health in about six months by studying the Six Healing Sounds. Learning how to defend oneself adequately might take a few years. The time required would be shorter than in most other systems because the techniques are used exactly the way they are practiced in this system.

chapter 2

A Hong Kong Southern Praying Mantis Cult
by Daniel M. Amos, Ph.D.

All photographs courtesy of D. Amos.

A Hong Kong Martial Arts Temple Cult

It has been observed that all social systems have a basis for power differentiation, and that "Power in all complex societies necessarily involves exploitation and may also involve marginalization" (Adams, 1974: 45). The leading group of every society attempts to maintain its position by exploiting subordinates, systematically withholding power from them (Adams, 1974: 45). While an authoritarian power elite may control a particular state and organize most activities, no single group in any society can organize every aspect of culture and society. In state-level societies, socially and politically marginal people are frequently able to form their own associations and engage in dramas of resistance against their situations in life.

Most of the individuals who engage in dramas of resistance do not think up the symbols of their resistance entirely by themselves. Through the process of socialization individuals learn about the cultural symbols that exist for the expression of resistance in their culture. The knight-errant has long been a symbol of resistance against oppression in Chinese culture (Liu, 1967). Hong Kong Chinese youths sometimes become knight-errants within the context of martial arts temple cults. The social structures of Hong Kong martial arts temple cults provide Chinese shunted aside by the dominant status system with an alternative, albeit secondary, system of status achievement.

Like Chinese secret societies in the past, contemporary Hong Kong martial arts temple cults offer a social background and a body politic in miniature through which martial artists find authority, protection, assistance, kinship, and through ritual, a measure of spiritual contentment (Lyman and Scott, 1975: 79). To participate in a martial arts temple cult Hong Kong youths must accept belief systems that are disreputable in the eyes of mainstream society. In Hong Kong the conscious models most disparaged by the power elite are those associated with the religious beliefs of the lowest social classes. Historically, Chinese religion has been socially hierarchical, and certain deities have been connected with specific social classes. Until the end of the Qing dynasty there were patron deities for scholars and magistrates, and for actors, Chinese opera performers, prostitutes, gamblers and martial artists (DeBernardi, 1983). DeBernardi (1983: 1) has noted that,

> The demise of the Ch'ing [Qing] dynasty left Confucius, the patron deity of the scholar-literati, largely neglected, and the City God's civic functions are no longer performed by a District Magistrate. The gods of the demi-monde, on the other hand, continue to command respect and to live in the imaginations of the urban poor.

In the 1960s, Frederick Wakeman wrote that martial arts brotherhoods gave boxing and sword fighting exhibitions in Tabei during religious festivals. He noted these associations were called "*fu-le she* and although their organization resembles that of a secret society they are known to the local authorities as correct sects (*cheng-pai*) and not as heterodox sects (*hsieh-pai*)" (Wakeman, 1966; quoted in Johnson, 1971: 185). The Hong Kong authorities are suspicious of martial arts brotherhoods and identify most of them as criminal Triad societies.

In 1976, I became associated with a Hong Kong gongfu temple cult. To protect the privacy of my informants I give the cult and its participants fictional names in this chapter. I call the cult the "True Descendent of the Bamboo Grove Temple of Jiangxi Province" (*Jiangxi Zhu Lin Si Zhen Zhuan*), lead by "Peng Zicheng's" disciple "Peng Weiyang" at the "'New Market Town' Praying Mantis Health Association" (*'Xin Ji Zhen' Tang Lang Jian Shen Hui*). I was introduced to Master Peng by middle-school classmates of his disciples, and was invited to join the cult in the autumn of 1976. The activities of the cult took place in a market town resettlement area in the New Territories and were centered in a martial house (*wu guan*) located in the master's apartment. According to Master Peng the cult originated in a Buddhist monastery, the Bamboo Grove Temple of Jiangxi Province, and the knowledge of the cult has been passed down through the generations to him. The master's followers stressed devotion to him. They expressed equalitarian values such as love and loyalty to "brothers" in the cult, yet there was a hierarchical social structure within the brotherhood, and the participants were doing more than simply "playing the game of structure."

The alternative structure of the gongfu cult was one attraction of the brotherhood for its members. They needed to experience high social status within structure, even if it was a secondary social structure of their own making, as much as persons with power occasionally need to escape the pressures of the dominant social structure (Turner, 1969). When interacting with one another the members of the cult moved from one modality to the other, from equalitarian anti-structure (Turner, 1969: 166-203) to hierarchical structure and back again (Gallimore, 1983). They played and joked with one another, but took the alternative hierarchy of the brotherhood seriously.

The brotherhood was dominated by Hakka (*kejia*), a distinct Han Chinese ethnic group of southern China. The term *Hakka* literally means "guest families" in Chinese. In a series of migrations originating in Jiangxi province during the eighteenth and nineteenth centuries, Hakka migrated to various parts of southern China and generally settled on inferior farm land (Spence, 1990: 169). Poorer and frequently marginalized, Hakka were seen as outsiders, and in the nineteenth and twentieth centuries they frequently led and participated in Chinese rebellions and revolutions. The various dialects and languages of the Hakka are unintelligible to the Cantonese, the dominant people of Guangdong province. In the nineteenth century a series of bloody wars was fought between these two ethnic groups (Spence, 1990: 169). During the latter twentieth century relations between Cantonese and Hakka have been peaceful, yet cultural differences remain.

Master Peng identifies with his Hakka heritage. While fluent in Cantonese, he speaks it with a slight Hakka accent. He preferred speaking

Hakka. In 1994 he explained the history of the Hakka people to me in the following way:

> Long ago, probably during the Tang dynasty (618-906), the Hakka people belonged to the Imperial Palace. After a change of dynasty they wandered and spread here and there. We were outsiders and called "guest families" by the native people, but we are not inferior to them. In fact, our language is much closer to Mandarin Chinese than the language of the local people here in Hong Kong.

Master Peng has been the leader of the New Market Town Praying Mantis gongfu cult for all of his adult life. He was born in 1942 in an isolated hamlet in the New Territories, where his lineage had resided since the time of the Qianlong Emperor (1736-1795). During the mid-1960s he and his kinsmen were forced to move again, this time to make way for a massive Hong Kong government public works project that destroyed their lineage lands and homes. In compensation, the government gave Master Peng and his kinsmen apartments in a tenement in a densely populated housing estate of "New Market Town." When Master Peng moved to New Market Town it had a population of twenty thousand people, but by 1976 the town's population had more than doubled. By 1994 it had a population of 500,000.

Coming from a small, single surname hamlet, Master Peng has been swept up in a process of social change. He has the demeanor and manners of a conservative peasant who makes his living from the soil. Better educated Hong Kongese who visit his martial house sometimes arrogantly call him a "hick" (*xiang xia lao*) behind his back. Master Peng feels that his situation in life was largely decided by his father's tragic fate during World War Two. During the Japanese occupation of Hong Kong his father was ordered to buy a bottle of wine by a Japanese soldier. When he did not respond quickly enough the soldier stabbed him. He died of his wounds a few months later. When his father was alive he earned his living by selling charcoal made from burning bushes on the hillsides surrounding the village. After his father's death the master and his mother were supported by relatives in the village, and by occasional work his mother found in the urban areas of Hong Kong. The master did not begin to speak Cantonese, the main Chinese language of Hong Kong, until the age of nine, his second year in school. He attended school for only three years. By the time he was eleven his mother was earning income assembling artificial flowers. The Hong Kong government did not subsidize elementary education at the time, and her income was not enough for her son to continue his studies. The master observed with regret that his formal education was shortened due to poverty:

School books were cheap back then, much cheaper than now. The most expensive were only two Hong Kong dollars apiece [approximately U.S. fifty cents in the 1950s]. But we were poor. We didn't have enough money to buy even these.

At the age of eleven Master Peng left school and worked as a deliverer of food for a Kowloon restaurant. Almost from the time he began working, he spent all of his spare time learning Southern Praying Mantis gongfu (*nan tang lang quan*) and *qilin* (sometimes inaccurately translated as "unicorn") dancing, when he was introduced to his master by his mother's younger brother. His master was also a Hakka, but not a member of his lineage. He was considered a distant relative only in so far as they shared the same surname. One of his master's most significant occupations was the practice of Chinese bonesetting. Chinese bonesetters (*dieda yisheng*) treat bruises, open wounds, rheumatism, lower back pain, general body aches, arthritis, sprains, dislocations, and fractures. Their medical treatments are the most popular form of Chinese medicine practiced in Hong Kong (Lee, 1975). Chinese bonesetting became part of Master Peng's training. By studying bonesetting he could improve his ability to recognize Chinese characters, because he was required to read and write the herbal remedies from his master's hand-copied Qing dynasty bonesetter manual. Master Peng said that his gongfu master was a strict disciplinarian.

> In the past if a gongfu disciple played around or was not modest toward his master and revealed a bad character by committing crimes, his master might lose his temper and kill his disciple. No one would blame him. My own master was really strict. If we did anything wrong he would beat us. Masters were almost like fathers in those days. If I made a wrong move he would hit me, and it would really hurt (rolls up pants leg to show scars).

Master Peng believes that Chinese martial artists in earlier times were more powerful and skilled than contemporary martial artists. This can be seen in his statements of 1979:

> In the old days boxers could carry heavy weights, they could carry weapons that weighed four and five hundred catties [440 to 550 pounds]. They would practice gongfu by carrying heavy weights. They would also strengthen their heads by knocking them against walls. They were very hard working. Today very few people are willing to work hard, so people aren't as strong as before.
>
> In the past if you tried to hit a boxer, you couldn't even touch him because his hands would move so fast. Some boxers were untouchable, they moved so quickly you couldn't even see them. My own master and 'elder gongfu uncle' (*shibo*) were very strong. Their arms were hard and their fists were deceptive. My elder gongfu uncle was in many fights with others who tried to test his gongfu ability. My elder gongfu uncle's hands were so powerful he could hold his fingers on the floor like a spider walking on the ground. Even if someone stamped on his fingers they would not move down to the floor. But more important than strength is skill. You Westerners say that strength is the most important, but we say skill. This is extremely significant!

My master and elder gongfu uncle were skilled in the internal points. Even I do not know them all. They were not willing to teach everything. It is extremely important to know the internal points because if you hit the right spot you can easily kill someone. You must also take precautions when practicing gongfu. To practice gongfu can also be dangerous.

Today many people who are practicing gongfu will die early because they do not practice it properly. If you do not breathe properly you will damage your internal organs. Also, if you are practicing gongfu and are hit with a hard blow it can damage your *qi* (internal energy within the body, a primal force). Therefore, you must take many precautions when practicing gongfu, but today few people even know how to breathe. In the past boxers knew many skills. For example, my elder gongfu uncle could suck his genitals up into his body so that they would be out of the way when he was fighting. Have you heard about this? There are many skills like this, but today few people know how to do them.

Master Peng believes that the variety of Southern Praying Mantis gongfu that he teaches is the most effective form of martial arts. He believes that even in the 1990s it is possible for one of his followers to become a skilled martial artist in five or six years. All that is required is diligent practice and dedication to his authority. If a boxer is not sincerely dedicated, even twenty years of practice is not long enough to learn the art. Clearly, Master Peng dedicated himself to following his master. When asked at what age he had decided to become a gongfu teacher he answered:

> I didn't really plan. My master told me to come out and teach. I wanted to study gongfu but I did not suspect what was going to happen. Therefore, I was surprised when my master asked me to begin teaching.

    Master Peng frequently says that Chinese martial arts masters will not allow their pupils to become gongfu teachers when they are too young for fear that "when they come out they will cause trouble and hurt their master's reputation." In spite of this statement, his own master invited him to begin teaching students at the age of nineteen. His first pupils were boys from his native hamlet and neighboring villages. In country villages like the master's native hamlet martial arts were quite useful. Gongfu cults provided defense against intruders, recreation for village boys, and performers for lineage rituals.

    When Master Peng and his kinsmen were forced to abandon their native village and relocate in New Market Town in the mid-1960s, he was in his early twenties. When he reopened his gongfu cult in his new apartment, he sent out announcements to relatives and local martial artists in the area. One local martial arts master perceived Master Peng's arrival as a threat. According to Master Peng, for over a year the rival master's disciples periodically attacked him and his disciples. Finally Master Peng and his followers beat their attackers in a decisive battle. After the last, violent encounter, detectives from the Hong Kong police interrogated Master Peng and his followers and took their photographs. Although he felt that the police were rude and ignorant, he convinced them that he was the aggrieved party, and the authorities did not take away his license to teach martial arts. This can be seen in his statements of the late 1970s:

> You know, many of my disciples, many young guys who do gongfu are called "delinquents" (*fei zai*) by people on the street. If someone doesn't know my disciples when he sees them on the street he would consider them delinquents. I ask you, "How do you know a delinquent?" Is it only by appearance? Only because they have long hair? Bad guys are not all long-haired. Some are always dressed up and have a good appearance, but the police call all the gongfu guys delinquents. The police used to just grab us and take us to jail. So we can't cooperate very well with the police in Hong Kong. Especially, when you consider that the police are always rude, harsh, and impolite. A few years ago they would just seize you and they would beat you. Several of them would just beat you up. Even today I am sometimes questioned and body-searched by them.
>
> They are only polite to foreigners. Now it has become better than before, because the people of Hong Kong have become wealthy. If the police put me in jail and beat me I can hire a lawyer or complain to the government. Especially after the I.C.A.C. (the Independent Commission Against Corruption) was established. No longer can the police force you to pay bribes. They all used to be completely corrupt. You always had to pay them brides. It was terrible. Now there is no more bribery. Still the Hong Kong police are really powerful and harsh. Did you read in the newspapers the other day how the Hong Kong police have the greatest power of any police in the world?

Although he has been the master of a gongfu cult for his entire adult life, Master Peng has not established a high reputation in the martial arts circles of Hong Kong. He has profited little from teaching gongfu. During the day he works as an assistant in a Kowloon noodle stand run by his mother and her partner. When he is not busy washing dishes and making Shanghai-style noodles by hand, he waits on the tables of workers who come in from the nearby factories for their midday meal. On returning to New Market Town from work the master invariably visits a local restaurant where he drinks beer and brandy and talks with friends. At 7:30 or 8:00 p.m. he returns to the martial house with bottles of wine and beer and awaits the arrival of his disciples.

Middle-class Chinese who visit his martial house invariably tell me that they feel that Master Peng is tall, thin, and unhealthy looking. They will guess that he is ten years older than his actual age. The master's appearance stems from heart disease exacerbated by alcoholism. Suffering from disease, the master is also a healer, a "bonesetting doctor" (*dieda yisheng*). In the past it was said in Hong Kong and Guangzhou that "you need to study bonesetting before you study martial arts." Some bonesetters in Hong Kong are well-known martial arts masters or even gongfu movie stars, but Master Peng is not famous. Most of his clients are his relatives and neighbors. They will give testimony to his ability to heal, and describe badly broken bones that he has successfully treated.

The Disciples of Master Peng

Every evening Monday through Saturday, at eight p.m., Master Peng's disciples (*tudi*) begin drifting into his apartment for gongfu practice. His disciples arrive and leave according to their own schedules, but even his closest disciples are usually gone by 10:15 p.m. Except the days preceding religious festivals when the members of the cult practice qilin dancing and stylized fighting routines, the master's disciples usually practice whatever gongfu routines they wish. Occasionally, the master orders an especially lazy disciple to practice a specific routine. During gongfu practice beginners are taught by more advanced disciples or by one of the master's four assistants. The master rarely takes notice of beginners, but he occasionally criticizes, punches, kicks, and teaches more experienced disciples. When the master teaches senior students he reveals segments of the blocking, punching, kicking, and grappling movements that are found in individual praying mantis boxing exercises. The dirty blue jeans, long sleeve shirt and plastic sandals that he wears do not inhibit his lanky grace. His movements are natural, unforced, yet complex and full of power. When he challenges senior disciples to spar, they invariably feel his sharp punches, blocks or kicks before their blows can reach his body.

Beginning disciples of the praying mantis gongfu cult are required to practice the basic posture and stance, the "horse stance" (*ma bu*), for at least four months before learning the first boxing exercise (*tao lu*). The horse stance helps to teach correct breathing, posture, stance and movement. Four versions of the horse stance are taught in the martial house before practice in the first boxing exercise begins. According to some Hong Kong martial artists, in the past it was necessary to practice the horse stance for three years before learning the first boxing exercise. Master Peng does not believe that this length of time is necessary for Southern Praying Mantis gongfu. This is shown in his comments of 1993:

> It is not necessarily true that all gongfu families used to require that much time to learn the horse stance. It depends on the family of gongfu that you practice. Hong Boxing, for example, requires a strong horse stance, so perhaps they need three years to learn the horse stance. Our boxing faction emphasizes liveliness and brightness, but you must practice praying mantis frequently. Of course, our horse stance must also be strong. If your foundation is bad, even if you are taught a whole set of gongfu it will be useless.

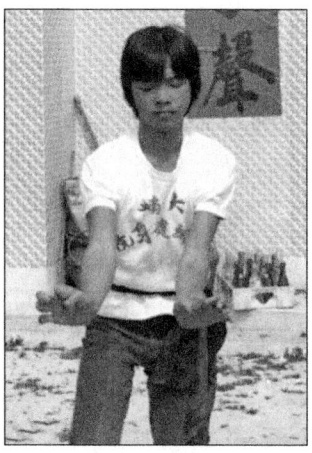

With the first exercise the beginner is taught to do paired punching and blocking exercises with a partner. These exercises not only perfect offensive and defensive movements, they also strengthen the boxers' wrists. The form of praying mantis gongfu practiced in the cult is inspired by the fighting style of the predatory insect *mantis religiosa*. This style of wushu makes extensive use of wrist blocks and attacks. Longtime practitioners of praying mantis develop large, rock-hard, bony knots around their wrists from constant micro-fracturing caused by striking their brothers' wrists during sparring exercises and by hitting trees and steel posts with their wrists. The wrist sparring exercises are painful, especially when they are done with experienced, battle hardened brothers. They provide for bruising rites of passage as they build weapons into the neophyte boxer's body.

The neophyte does not begin to recognize the function of the movements of the first boxing exercises until he or she has done extensive sparring. The first exercise involves a series of hand and knee movements that function as blocks and attacks in combat. The second boxing exercise is complex and involves leg blocks and two-handed punching. This second form is generally learned at the end of the first year. The third and fourth forms are learned during the second and third years. Study of the fifth form, the most complex weaponless exercise, may begin during the third year of practice or even a few years later. The first weapon form is taught to diligent disciples during the second year. Devoted followers of the master learn thirty six weapon routines after five years. After this time, a serious disciple also knows sixteen kinds of qilin dances and some elements of Chinese bonesetting.

In 1976 when I first asked how many gongfu disciples followed him, Master Peng stated "thousands and thousands." The following year, he said that he was in direct contact with only a few hundred disciples. Since 1973 the Hong Kong authorities have required private martial arts masters to have licenses, to pay an annual fee, and to make a public record of their disciples. To fulfill this requirement martial arts masters must take down the names and addresses of their disciples and collect two photos from each disciple, one for their own records and another for the police. By 1977 Master Peng had collected the names, addresses, and photos of 94 disciples, and by 1981, 153 disciples were listed in his register. In 1994 his register held 277 names. Because he has not achieved a high reputation in Hong Kong martial arts circles, Master Peng's tuition fees are lower than those of many martial arts masters.

In 1977, Hakka followers of Master Peng who were not his close disciples paid him thirty Hong Kong dollars (approximately U.S. $5.00 in 1977) per month. Chinese from other ethnic groups paid him forty Hong Kong dollars. These rates contrasted with fees of fifty to two hundred Hong Kong dollars per month charged by other local martial arts masters. In 1994 Hakka followers paid Master Peng one hundred Hong Kong dollars per month, and Cantonese followers paid him one hundred and fifty Hong Kong dollars.

Master Peng has three kinds of disciples: relatives who follow him in the cult, dedicated disciples who practice gongfu with him and become involved in the cult, and students who pay for their gongfu lessons but do not become deeply involved in the cult. As is generally customary in Hong Kong, Master Peng's relatives and closest disciples do not pay tuition fees. Instead, they perform favors for the master and sometimes give him gifts of cash. All but one of the master's closest followers is a fellow Hakka. Like the master, most come from the lower social classes. His followers are mostly unmarried youths, or less commonly, working class men with wives and families. By establishing a relationship with Master Peng and through him mastering a religion of the body, sworn disciples of the master achieve status and experience "structure" within a social grouping of their own making. Simultaneously, they gain confidence in their ability to strengthen their bodies and dominate others.

Kinship and Fictive Kinship Within the Cult

In both Hong Kong and Guangzhou the structural basis of many social hierarchies formed by martial artists is a fictive kinship system. The term *shi*, which can be translated to mean "master" or "teacher," shows a fictive kin relationship and is added in front of most terms of address. The martial arts master is called *shifu*. Shifu is written with two characters *shi* and *fu*, and the second character *fu* can be written with two different characters that are homophones. A literal translation of the most common form of the expression *shifu* is "teacher-father." An alternate form is translated "master craftsman." In Master Peng's cult the former form was used. While Chinese kinship is patrilineal, the fictive kinship system associated with Chinese martial arts has an extra male supremacist bias. Female martial artists from generations earlier than oneself are addressed by masculine kin terms. For example, women who were fellow students with one's master are called *shibo* (elder uncle) or *shishu* (younger uncles). The fictive kinship terminology of Chinese martial arts groups can be diagrammed in the following manner:

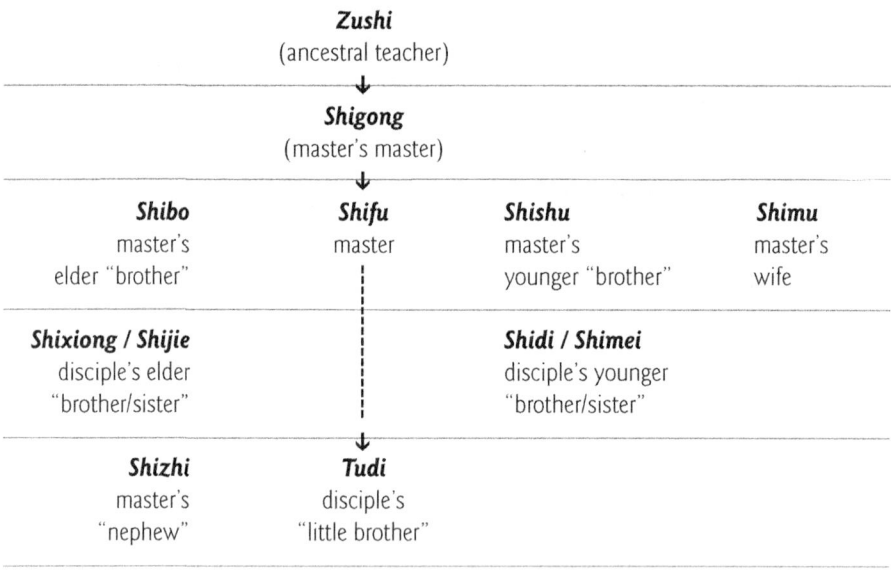

Within Master Peng's gongfu cult there is a merging of kin and fictive kin relationships. Fictive kin of Master Peng have achieved significant positions within his cult, although a consanguineous or affinal relationship to the master is an important factor in deciding a boxer's standing in the gongfu cult, especially since members of the cult are involved in the religious celebrations of the master's kinsmen. Master Peng's cult is a socio-religious entity that consists of two ritual organizations. Internally there is the cult of gongfu boxers, where fictive kin hold high positions. Externally there is a welfare association where members of the master's lineage hold positions more important than the master's disciples.

Seniority determines a boxer's standing. Longtime followers of the master have higher positions than newcomers. Disciples with consanguineous or affinal ties to the master take precedent over disciples without such ties. In 1978 the boxer who was the most important follower of Master Peng was not a relative. He was the master's first assistant, his childhood friend and first follower. The second assistant was ten years younger than the master. He was the master's agnate (same father's father), and second gongfu disciple. The third assistant, eleven years younger than the master, was a member of the master's lineage and had been a disciple of the master since the age of ten. The fourth assistant was related to the master by marriage (wife's father's younger brother's first daughter). By 1978 she had followed the master for eight years.

The welfare association attached to the gongfu cult is called Master Peng Weiyang's Golden Pork Association (*Jin Ru Hui*). Master Peng serves as chairman of the Golden Pork Association and through the association he involves his gongfu disciples in the religious celebrations of his lineage. In 1978 the master named seven of his agnates to the directorship, the highest positions in the association. The First Director was the senior *fu lao* (elder) from the master's native village. Another director was the master's father's eldest brother. The seventh and lowest ranking director was his father's eldest brother's first son. This last relative was the youngest of the master's agnates on the board of directors, and was the only director who attended association meetings. The highest ranking person in the association who was not Peng's relative was a man fifteen years older than the master. He was the master's "elder gongfu brother" (*shixiong*). He was named Co-Chairman of the association. The master's first assistant was named Vice Chairman. The master's second assistant simultaneously served as Second Vice Chairman, Treasurer, and First Secretary of the association. The third assistant served as Third Vice Chairman and Second Secretary. The fourth assistant and her paternal parallel cousin were named Assistant Treasurers. Three longtime disciples of the master were named Third Secretary, Fourth Secretary, and Fifth Secretary, respectively. An English speaking disciple of the master was named Secretary for English Translation.

All of the master's closest followers belonged to the Golden Pork Association, but not everyone who practiced martial arts under his direction joined the association. Only those disciples who were willing to become involved in the religious celebrations of the master's lineage, spent additional time with their "gongfu brothers" and paid additional membership fees (approximately U.S. $2.00 per month in 1978), joined the association. In 1978 the activities of the association involved fifty-six of the seventy-one boxers who actively trained with the master that year. In addition, fourteen disciples who were not actively training with the master participated in the religious celebrations connected with the cult.

The religious celebrations that concerned the Golden Pork Association included the Chinese Lunar New Year festivities, the festivities associated with the Mid-Autumn Festival and the celebrations associated with the festival for Tian Hou (Empress of Heaven, a goddess who protects fishermen, who was worshiped by the Peng lineage because many of the villagers earned their living by fishing). A religious ritual that the gongfu cult participated in, but which did not involve the Golden Pork Association, was the Chong Yang Festival, one of the two Chinese festivals for the dead. During the Chong Yang Festival, the gongfu cult worshiped at the tomb of Master Peng's gongfu master. Another activity associated with the cult's qilin dance team comprised the spirit possession rites that maintained and transferred the qilin's spirit. The *qilin*, a legendary animal whose appearance is regarded as auspicious, is one of the four great mythical creatures of Chinese culture, the others being the dragon, the phoenix, and the tortoise.

There are various descriptions of the auspicious qilin. It has been described as having ". . . the tail of an ox, fishy scales, cloven toes or five toes to each foot, and a horn covered with fur" (Eberhard, 1988: 303). It has also been said that its body is like that of a musk deer, with the hooves of a horse, the forehead of a wolf and the tail of an ox (Au, 1980). Its skin has five colors: red, yellow, blue, black, and white, expressing lively feelings (Au, 1980). Another description of the qilin gives the creature a body of a horse with scales and two horns bent backwards. The qilin is sometimes called a dragon horse (*long ma*) (Huang, 1986). According to Master Peng every qilin, including those portrayed by martial artists in dance costume, has either a male or a female spirit. The male is the *qi* and the female is the *lin* in "qilin." According to some descriptions, male qilins have at least one horn protruding from the forehead, while females have none. The qilin is represented by Buddhists as carrying on its back the civilizing *Book of Law* (Au, 1980; Huang, 1986). A dragon horse is recorded to have come out of the Yellow River and appeared to the first legendary Emperor Fuxi, bearing on its back a mystic map from which Chinese writing is said to have evolved (Au, 1980; Huang, 1986).

Besides the ritual festivities already mentioned, the members of the gongfu cult who belong to the Golden Pork Association go on holiday excursions to the outlying islands of Hong Kong such as Lantau Island and the neighboring Portuguese colony of Macau. In the 1990s they visited the neighboring city of Shenzhen in the People's Republic of China. The association holds ten meetings per year to prepare and plan for religious and recreational activities. The meetings occasionally coincide with farewell parties for members of the brotherhood leaving Hong Kong to study or work overseas. Like many other common interest associations in Chinese culture, Master Peng's Golden Pork Association has many offices and positions that make it possible for every active member to have an official title. Less important members are given positions such as Director or Vice-Director of Entertainment, a position that involves buying food and provisions for the meetings and excursions of the association. In the past my own title was Association Photographer. For a few years I was the only one of Master Peng's followers who possessed a camera. As part of my duties I provided a photographic record of the cult's activities.

An Ideology of Equality & A Reality of Structure

If one were to judge from the ideology of Master Peng's gongfu cult alone, one could assume that the socially inferior members of the cult had united in a state of equality to escape the pressures of social structure (Turner, 1969). Senior members of the cult would frequently say, "We are all 'brothers' here. There are no 'big brothers' or 'small brothers'." In reality, there was a continuous hierarchy of power within the alternative structure of the gongfu cult. A boxer's power was determined by his relationship to Master Peng. The most prominent principle in deciding one's relationship to the Master was seniority. The longer a boxer had been a dedicated disciple of Master Peng, the more likely he was to have authority in the cult. This means that a boxer who had studied with the master for a few months less than another boxer was technically required to address him as elder brother (*da shixiong*). Therefore, one attraction of the cult to adolescent boys, besides learning how to fight well, was that the benefits of seniority rapidly accumulated.

Over a span of a couple of years a few senior boxers in the cult would emigrate overseas or marry and cease participating in the cult. At the same time, many more new disciples would begin learning gongfu. A boy might thus find himself rapidly advancing in status. Fewer senior boxers would be present to order him around and many newcomers would be required to follow his instructions. The boxers were also aware that if they were diligent in practicing gongfu and in following Master Peng's instructions, they would be rewarded with more prestigious offices in the Golden Pork Association. The association represented the intermingling of dominant kin and other social structures with the alternative internal structure of the gongfu cult itself. Even extremely diligent, long time disciples of the master had little hope of being named to the highest positions in the association however, because these positions were reserved for men of high standing in the master's lineage.

Among his own kinsmen it was evident that Master Peng was held in low regard. Most of the men to whom the master had given the highest titles in his association had little to do with its functioning. These men perceived that Master Peng's gongfu cult was useful to the extent that it provided performers for the ritual functions of the lineage. However, the master's service to his lineage gained him little merit among his kinsmen.

In contrast to the senior members of his lineage, the gongfu cult was significant to the lives of Master Peng's disciples. Few of them belonged to other voluntary associations and most took their duties within the cult seriously. This seriousness of purpose was shown in 1979, two weeks after the Mid-Autumn Festival. The Autumn Festival, which occurs on the fifteenth day of the eighth month of the Chinese calendar, is characterized in Hong Kong by worship of the moon, drinking, feasting, and the exchange and consumption of moon cakes. Moon cakes are a golden brown pastry that may be stamped on top with Chinese characters denoting their ingredients. The cakes are filled with a variety of tasty treats that may include sugared beans, lotus seeds, sesame, eggs, nuts, and sometimes meat and sausage (Berkowitz 1969; Eberhard 1988).

During the night of the festival the cult performed gongfu and did the qilin dance in the community square that stood in the center of the five story Hong Kong government-constructed tenements that the master's lineage was resettled in. During the night of the Mid-Autumn Festival in 1979, Wang Xiaotong, Fifth Secretary of the Golden Pork Association, and his younger brother Wang Xiaodun did not participate in the performance as they had promised. A week after the festival there was a meeting of the Golden Pork Association. The meeting was held for three reasons: to discipline the errant Wang brothers, to celebrate the promotion of Beauty Boxer to the position of fourth assistant, and to send off Little Cop, the third assistant, who was scheduled to leave Hong Kong in six days to work and possibly to settle permanently in Northern Ireland.

At eight in the evening the meeting of the Golden Pork Association was opened by Hunchback, a longtime disciple of the master and his close friend. Thirty-five brothers, aged ten to thirty-four, were packed into the four hundred square foot section of the master's apartment that served as the martial house. The Wang brothers were not present.

The first activity was to invite the elder brothers (*da shi xiong*) of the association to show their gongfu. Nine disciples of the master, aged twenty-two to thirty-four, were chosen to display their martial skill. I was the last person selected. Little Cop performed first. He did a clean, beautiful version of the second gongfu exercise taught to first year disciples within the cult. Beauty Boxer was then invited to perform. She did a flawless set of Six and a Half (*liu dian ban*), a fighting stick exercise taught during the second or third year of diligent practice.

After nine senior disciples of Master Peng had demonstrated their gongfu, eight rectangular folding tables were placed together to make one large, long table. The room was smoke-filled, as most disciples over the age of thirteen were smoking. San Miguel Beer, soda, pastry and peanuts were served as refreshments. Elder Brother Hong, the first assistant to Master Peng, directed the discussion. During the meeting the discipline within the martial house was severe, in contrast to the lax, lighthearted attitude prevalent during gongfu practice. Little Cop sternly ordered me not to drop empty peanut shells on the floor (the usual practice). Other senior disciples of the master kept tight discipline over junior disciples. Master Peng simply sat back in his chair. He said nothing, but occasionally nodded his head. Non-action was his greatest symbol of authority.

Elder Brother Hong and Little Cop began the discourse by discussing whether the Wang brothers should be expelled from the Golden Pork Association, or merely given a warning. Elder Brother Hong and Little Cop both complained that the Wangs had promised to be at the Mid-Autumn Festival, but had failed to present themselves for the performance of the Golden Pork Association before Master Peng's lineage. This was a serious insult to Master Peng and a bad example to other brothers in the association. Elder Brother Hong then asked six of the younger, junior members of the brotherhood what the association should do: "Should we expel the two Wang brothers or should we be lenient?" Four said that the association should be lenient and forgive them. Two said that the Wangs should be expelled.

Elder Brother Hong then asked Master Peng what the Golden Pork Association should do. In a few words the master said that if the association decided to expel the brothers he would not let the Wang brothers practice praying mantis gongfu at the martial house. Elder Brother Hong repeated that it was a serious matter that two longtime members of the association had broken their promise to the master.

In the middle of Elder Brother Hong's speech, nearly one hour after the meeting had begun, the younger of the two Wang brothers, a fifteen-year-old middle-school student, walked into the martial house. He seemed to be unaware of the nature of the meeting taking place and he appeared to have come to the martial house merely to practice gongfu. He looked for a place to sit near the far end of the table, away from the seats of honor. Elder Brother Hong directed him to stand and face the senior brothers sitting at the middle of the table. As Young Wang walked toward the middle of the table he tripped over a box of soft drinks and Elder Brother Hong said, "Help yourself to a drink." Elder Brother Hong then asked Young Wang why he was late for the meeting. Why had he and his brother failed to come to the Mid-Autumn Festival performance of gongfu when they had promised to participate? When Elder Brother Hong spoke, Young Wang looked at the floor. Everyone else was silent and tense. Elder Brother Hong continued, "If you promise to come to an event of our association but then cannot come, say, for example, you are not free or you have to help your father or to study for school, then telephone the martial house beforehand and tell us that you're not coming."

Elder Brother Hong again asked three of the newer members what the association should do with the two Wang brothers. One said that he did not know. The other two said that the Wang brothers should be given another chance, but that they should perform their duties properly in the future. At this point Elder Brother Hong turned to Young Wang and said, "You can continue to come to the association, but you must act properly in the future. You must attend all the functions and inform the association when you cannot come. Telephone if you are busy." Wang was then allowed to sit and the matter was resolved after the association had taken over an hour to discuss the issue.

Hunchback, the master's close friend and disciple, then said that the next issue was the announcement of Beauty Boxer's appointment as the master's new assistant. He asked Beauty Boxer to say a few words and everyone looked in her direction. She stood up, looked at her feet and turned red. Elder Brother Hong encouraged her to speak but she was not able to say anything. Hunchback then turned to Little Cop, the master's third assistant, and said, "Little Cop, the master's old disciple, one of our great elder brothers, is soon going to be leaving for Ireland to work and study. Won't you say a few words for us?" Little Cop was fond of public speaking and he did not hesitate to address the association:

> Under the master we are all the same. We are brothers. Soon I will be going abroad after following the master's instruction for many years. It's hard to express what I feel. The master has helped me in many, many ways. He has been my teacher, and has taught me every valuable thing that I know. He has allowed me be his disciple. I have followed him for many years. He has taught me praying mantis gongfu and many other things. I don't know how to repay him. I cannot ever repay him. I can only say one thing to the master. I can only say, "Thank you."

The brothers were moved by Little Cop's words and his speech went on for some time. When he finished there was loud applause. Following the speech the master gave Little Cop a present from the association, a gold-plated cigarette lighter. After accepting the gift Little Cop invited Little Champ, another member of the Peng lineage and the master's second assistant, to speak. Little Champ laughed, as was usual when asked to speak at the meetings of the association. He rose to his feet and said that he did not have anything to say, except that he hoped that Little Cop would be successful in Ireland. He, too, thanked the master for his teachings.

Little Cop and Hunchback again asked Beauty Boxer to address the association. She stood up but looked downward and haltingly said, "I wish to thank the Master for allowing me to follow him and for helping me. I want to thank my gongfu brothers as well." She then sat down again.

The master remained in his seat but spoke directly to Little Cop. He said that if Little Cop was thinking about leading new martial arts followers overseas, he would consider allowing him to open a branch of the association in Ireland when the proper time came and when Little Cop made the appropriate formal request. Master Peng said that if he allowed Little Cop to open a new branch of the praying mantis cult in Ireland, Little Cop would have to set up the proper shrines and the Irish followers would be required to worship and to pay respect to the ancestral master in Hong Kong. Little Cop's Irish followers would be considered disciples of the ancestral master and Master Peng.

At 10:20 p.m. the tables were folded and moved back. Recently chastised Young Wang was the first disciple to formally ask the master's permission to leave the martial house for the night and permission was granted. Elder Brother Hong then invited Little Cop to display his martial skill again. Little Cop took off his shirt and performed the most difficult boxing routine of praying mantis gongfu. He moved naturally and with precision. Each punch and block was delivered with such authority and speed that the movement of his hands made audible sounds. As Little Cop boxed the senior disciples of the master shouted out words of encouragement and when he finished they applauded and yelled, "Great!"

As a special honor to Little Cop, Elder Brother Hong offered to do *shen da*, a form of spirit possession. Elder Brother Hong said that he was simply playing at shen da, not doing the real thing. He said he was performing in order for us to better remember the events of the evening. Elder Brother removed his shirt and began to stagger around the room as though intoxicated, breathing deeply and closing his eyes. He walked backwards in a counter-clockwise direction doing what appeared to be a form of Drunken Boxing, repeatedly writing a Chinese character on the palm of his left hand with his right forefinger and circling it. He took a large, heavy, meat cleaver from Hyena. Using the broadside of the cleaver, he hit himself three times on the chest and with the sharp edge of the blade he struck himself with three quick, forceful chops to his diaphragm. The blows only left red marks on his skin. Elder Brother Hong's performance was rewarded by shouts and wild applause from his brothers.

Other elder brothers were invited to perform: Little Champ, Beauty Boxer, Hyena, Hunchback, Lili, Wild Stuttering Jap, Fatty, and myself. I did the second praying mantis exercise, and as I boxed my brothers shouted to me, "Punch harder! Breathe naturally! Don't breathe so hard! Don't breathe through your mouth! Harder!" Although the boxers in the cult are not hierarchically ranked with belts, practice and performance in front of brothers make obvious a boxer's level of skill.

After the elder brothers' gongfu demonstrations, Elder Brother Hong asked Sissy Peng, the master's twelve year old paternal cousin (*tang xiong di*), to perform. The master was critical of Sissy Peng and the master's criticism and physical punishment frequently caused him to cry. Sissy Peng did the first gongfu exercise and during his performance the exhortations of his brothers were the same as those shouted at me. When Sissy Peng finished Elder Brother Hong said, "Not bad," and the other brothers applauded. The rest of the master's disciples were then ordered to do gongfu, and the younger brothers did the first praying mantis exercise in pairs across the martial house floor. The gongfu demonstrations in honor of Master Peng, Little Cop and Beauty Boxer lasted until 11:10 p.m. Then most of the brothers formally asked permission of the master to leave the martial house. After that night neither of the two Wang brothers ever set foot in the martial house again. A few months later, ten days before the Lunar New Year festivities, a statement was attached to the cult's bulletin board. It read:

> This welfare association has decided to have qilin dancing on the sixteenth and seventeenth of February, 1980, the first and second days of the Lunar New Year. All disciples must present themselves to the association at eight in the morning and set off at nine. All those who cannot join the procession please report to the master within three days from the date of this notice. Otherwise, there will be severe punishment.

Changes in the Cult from 1980 to 1994

Significant changes occurred in Master Peng's martial house after the Lunar New Year's festivities of 1980. In 1981 Master Peng reported that new laws enacted by the Hong Kong government regarding Lion and Qilin dance teams adversely affected him and the martial house,

> When I want my disciples to do the qilin dance I have to apply to the police. I have to give them my [Hong Kong] identity card number and give the government sponsored insurance company $5,000 H.K. as a bond and then pay them $80.00 H.K. more for an insurance policy. If the police accuse us of causing any trouble we lose the $5,000 H.K. They convict you even before you begin! We're not going to do the qilin dance this year during the Mid-Autumn Festival. It's too expensive and too troublesome. Maybe we will dance for our neighbors and our relatives in the square below the martial house, but not elsewhere. It's too much trouble to apply for a license. We are bitter about this. The Hong Kong government is too unreasonable. They are always making trouble for martial houses.

By 1983 Elder Brother Hong was no longer the master's first assistant. He and the master had had a falling out and Elder Brother Hong did not return to the martial house. When the master mentioned Elder Brother Hong he accused him of arrogance and disloyalty.

Elder Brother Hong's position as first assistant had been taken by Little Champ, but Little Champ had married and by 1985 he was the father of a two-year-old boy. Little Champ only found time to participate in the cult during the meetings of the Golden Pork Association and during the training and practice sessions leading up to the major festivals such as the Lunar New Year.

By 1985 Hunchback was also estranged from Master Peng. He was still employed as a fireman, but his chronically aching lower back was no longer treated at Master Peng's bonesetting clinic.

Hick was long gone from the martial house. In the late 1970s he had joined a criminal Triad Society and was arrested in 1980 after attempting to extort money from a mini-van driver. Master Peng was visited by the Hong Kong police after Hick's arrest, but the master explained that Hick no longer practiced gongfu at his martial house. Scholar practiced gongfu at the martial house for less than a year and quit after finding employment with a Hong Kong computer firm. He neither maintained ties with the master nor with members of the cult.

By 1985 Fatty only occasionally practiced gongfu at the martial house, but he continues to participate in the ritual festivities of the cult up to the present. Both his parents are dead and he and his wife have remained childless. He returns to practice at the martial house when longtime brothers like me visit Hong Kong. As my original sponsor and immediate superior in the martial house he still gives me directions and corrects the faults in my gongfu form when I return to take gongfu instruction from Master Peng. He is even fatter than when I first met him in 1976, but he remains a competent and agile martial artist.

In 1985 Master Peng observed that I was fatter but stronger, and he reminded me how shallow my knowledge of praying mantis gongfu was. When he instructed me in 1994 he said that I was a better boxer when I was younger. He complained that my form is steadily deteriorating.

Hyena has remained Master Peng's devoted follower and close friend. In 1984 he became the owner of a popular working class tavern in New Market Town. Master Peng generally avoided the tavern, because local Triad members and delinquents hung out at Hyena's bar and fights were frequent. Hyena sold the bar in 1991, but used his profits to invest in real estate. A success at business, Hyena's courtship of Beauty Boxer was also successful and they married in 1983. By 1985 she was a busy mother and housewife, and had neither the time nor the desire to be Master Peng's assistant. She still considered herself the master's student, but she and her cousin Lili had retired from active participation in the martial house.

Peng Deying remained an active member of the Golden Pork Association. Employed as a clerk in a local supermarket, Deying frequently can be found smoking cigarettes and conversing with cult brothers at the martial house.

Wild Stuttering Jap, Deying's younger brother, can also be found at the martial house. In spite of the master's vow many years earlier, by 1985 Wild Stuttering Jap had become the master's second assistant. He had become reliable. By 1985 he was the father of a daughter and two sons. He worked at his father-in-law's liquor store and had developed an interest in doing business. In 1994 he had a position as a maintenance worker at a local power company. He weighs fifty pounds more than in the mid-1970s, but is still a graceful, powerful martial artist.

Almost every evening Wild Stuttering Jap attends to the duties of the martial house and he has become a conscientious assistant of Master Peng. He derives less pleasure from his nickname, but within the cult he cannot shake it. Unlike Master Peng he has traveled extensively in mainland China, and he visited me when I worked in Guangzhou and Beijing. He also makes shorter trips to neighboring Shenzhen, where he frequents houses of prostitution.

By 1985 Rubber Arms no longer participated in the activities of the martial house, and the last anyone heard he was still drinking heavily and working in a dress shop.

Master Peng had fallen out with Killer King, his younger gongfu brother who was active in the cult in the late seventies. Killer King never became a barrister or even graduated from middle-school, yet he managed to become a successful salesman of office furniture. According to senior disciples in the cult, Master Peng believed that Killer King had become arrogant and untrustworthy and the master had severed all connection with him.

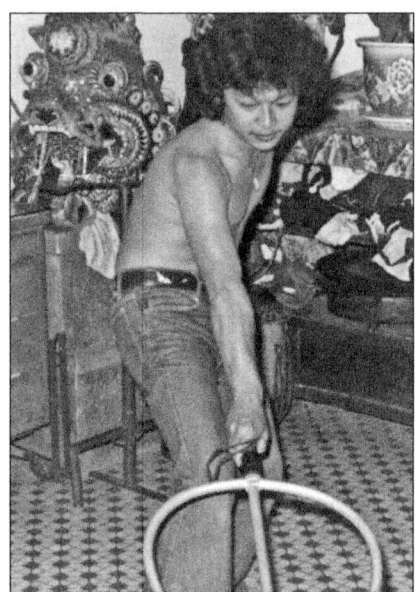

Crazy Godfather still had ties with some of his gongfu brothers and with some of Master Peng's disciples, but not with Master Peng. After living with him off and on for twenty years Crazy Godfather quarreled with Master Peng and moved out of the martial house. In 1994 he was working as a door watchman at an office building in an industrial section of Kowloon.

Little Cop, Master Peng's third assistant in 1978, had moved to Derry (Londonderry), Northern Ireland in 1979. He married a Catholic Irish woman and became the father of four children. Little Cop opened his own martial house in Derry in 1984, but neglected to ask Master Peng's formal approval beforehand. In 1985 Little Cop's gongfu brothers claimed that he had become a successful praying mantis master. Several brothers had received snapshots showing Little Cop surrounded by the boys and tall bearded Irishmen who had become his gongfu disciples. Master Peng said little about Little Cop except to suggest that he considered him unfilial and disloyal. By 1994 Little Cop and the master had reconciled. Little Cop returned to Hong Kong to spend the Chinese Lunar New Year with his relatives. He spent New Year Eve gambling with Master Peng at the martial house.

When Little Champ danced the head of the qilin in 1980, ten year old Huang Kaiping danced the tail. Kaiping entered Master Peng's gongfu cult at the age of nine when he was introduced to the master by his father, a former patient of Master Peng who was impressed by the master's ability to heal. From the day that he joined the cult Kaiping had been an enthusiastic follower of Master Peng and a dedicated disciple of praying mantis gongfu. By 1985 he had become a superb martial artist and qilin dancer. The master was slowly revealing to Kaiping the secrets of Chinese bonesetting. Kaiping did some of the more mundane aspects of therapeutic treatments such as massaging the pressure points of the master's patients with herbal medicine. Kaiping had completed Form Four in a mediocre Chinese language Middle School and hoped to find employment as a postal clerk. By 1994 he had married and lessened his involvement with the master's martial arts cult.

Master Peng's life had also changed. In 1982 he had an operation to repair a faulty heart valve. He continued to drink heavily, but since the operation he had gained weight and his complexion had taken on a healthier color. In 1985 he explained his approach to medical treatment and practice:

> I went to a western physician for the surgery because western medicine is better for life-threatening emergencies. Chinese medicine is better for treating broken bones, bruises, wounds and chronic conditions such as arthritis and lower back pain, but western medicine is better for emergencies. It's true, I also use western medicine. For example, when my patients have a fracture, I ask them to go get an X-ray so that I can analyze and treat the problem. After I get the X-ray I can set the fracture, make the wrappings, and prescribe the bonesetting medicines for healing. Chinese bonesetting is superior to western medicine in treating broken bones, but western medicine can also help the process. But if you foreigners break your foot, you wrap it for a long time in a plaster cast. This causes rheumatism in old age. Chinese medicine will cure it completely without any problems in the future. Chinese medicine cures all diseases completely. Once I had a patient who could not be cured by a western doctor. He came to see me. I gave him some Chinese medicine and told him that he would vomit blood after taking it. He followed my instructions and under my care he was healed at last.

Changes also occurred in Master Peng's marriage and family life. In 1983 his marriage ended when he accused his wife of committing adultery. After the divorce he retained custody of their four children and raised them with the assistance of his still handsome seventy-year-old mother. When his marriage ended Master Peng began to play a more active role in the upbringing of his children. He began to escort his youngest daughter to school and to make sure that his children completed their homework. The master's eldest child, his teenage daughter, did well in school. She was also an excellent martial artist and could perform the qilin dance. When asked in 1989 if he would choose her to become a martial arts master, Master Peng answered,

> If she is sincere and diligent in her practice of Southern Praying Mantis gongfu and she does not want to use it for selfish purposes, she may be chosen. However, I would prefer that she attend university.

This was a realistic assessment. It is likely that she would have a more respectable career as a university graduate than as a martial arts master ordained by her father. By 1994 she had neither attended university nor become a martial arts master. She has become a serious amateur softball player and travels to compete with teams throughout Southeast Asia and mainland China.

In 1989 Master Peng was especially concerned about the future of his son. The master complained that his son was lazy and doing poorly in school, and he chastised him for not working hard enough at perfecting his gongfu. In front of his son Master Peng informed his disciples that he would never allow his son to become a martial arts master. In reality, his son's gongfu was already quite good. When he was being publicly castigated by his father he merely smiled. The master's assistants had already told him that one day he too would become a master. However, by 1994 he was completely out of his father's favor. He had only completed Form Four in middle-school and was unemployed. "He's worthless," said Master Peng.

By 1994 gongfu appeared to be less popular with Hong Kong youth than it had been in the 1970s and 1980s. Master Peng taught one-fourth the number of students that he had taught in earlier times. His explanation for the decline of his martial arts house is revealed in a statement he made in 1994:

> During the time of Bruce Lee, gongfu was really popular in Hong Kong. When he died there was a great gongfu "heat." Everyone wanted to be a martial hero like Bruce Lee. I have told you that I really don't know how good he was. I know that he didn't master Yong Chun gongfu. His master and fellow students have said this, but nobody knows how good he became when he invented his own style of martial arts. His technique was not as effective as praying mantis gongfu, but he was very fast and strong. He was small and had fast hands and really fast feet. He made gongfu popular in Hong Kong. Bruce Lee has been dead for a long time now. The gongfu in the movies today is totally false. None of the actors really knows martial arts any more. Gongfu has been destroyed by movies.

It is a joke. These days all the young guys are too spoiled and lazy to learn gongfu. Hong Kong has become too rich. It is too troublesome to teach these spoiled kids. They are not like we were. They know nothing about desire, discipline, sacrifice, and loyalty. Gongfu is everything. It is life. I will only accept a few, dedicated disciples. I will not waste my time.

Glossary of Chinese Terms

Chong² Yang²	重陽	Mid-Autumn Festival
da² shi¹ xiong¹	大師兄	master elder brother
die¹ da³ yi¹ sheng¹	跌打醫生	Chinese bonesetter; osteopath
gong¹ fu¹ (kungfu)	功夫	(martial) skill
Jin¹ Rou⁴ Hui⁴	金肉會	Golden Pork Association
ke⁴ jia¹	客家	Hakka (guest family)
liu⁴ dian³ ban⁴	六點半	Six and a Half (fighting stick form)
ma³ bu⁴	馬步	basic "horse" stance/step
Nan² Tang² Lang² Quan²	南螳螂拳	Southern Praying Mantis Boxing
qi² lin²	麒麟	a supernatural creature
shi¹ bo²	師伯	master's elder martial brother
shi¹ di⁴	師第	master's younger martial brother
shi¹ fu⁴	師父	master
shi¹ gong¹	師公	master's master
shi¹ jie³	師姐	disciple's elder martial sister
shi¹ mei⁴	師妹	disciple's younger martial sister
shi¹ mu³	師母	master's wife
shi¹ shu¹	師叔	master's younger martial brother
shi¹ xiong¹	師兄	disciple's elder martial brother
shi¹ zhi¹	師姪	master's martial nephew/niece
tao⁴ lu⁴	套路	first boxing form ("trapping way")
Tian¹ Hou¹	天后	Empress of Heaven
tu² di⁴	徒第	disciple of the master
tu² sun¹	徒孫	martial grandson (disciple's disciple)
wu³ guan³	武館	martial house (hall)
wu³ shu²	武術	martial arts
xiang¹ xia⁴ lao³	鄉下佬	country "hick"
Yong³ Chun¹ (Wing Chun)	詠春	Radiant Spring
zu³ shi¹	祖師	ancestral master

Bibliography

Adams, R. and Fogelson, R. (Eds.). (1974). *Harnessing technological development: The anthropology of power*. New York: Academic Press.

Au, K. (1980). Personal communication to the author.

Berkowitz, M., Brandauer, F., and Reed, J. (1969). *Folk religion in an urban setting*. Hong Kong: Christian Study Centre on Chinese Religion and Culture.

Brownell, S. (1995). *Training the body for China: Sports in the moral order of the People's Republic*. Chicago: University of Chicago Press.

DeBernardi, J. (1983, March). *The god of war and the vagabond Buddha: Symbolic aspects of social marginality in Penang's black societies*. Paper presented at the 35th Annual Meeting of the Association for Asian Studies.

Eberhard, W. (1988). *A dictionary of Chinese symbols: Hidden symbols in Chinese life and thought*. New York: Routledge.

Gallimore, R. (1983). Personal communication to the author.

Huang, J. (1986). Personal communication to the author.

Johnson, G. (1971). *Natives, migrants, and voluntary associations in a colonial setting*. Unpublished doctoral dissertation, University of California, Los Angeles.

Liu, J. (1967). *The Chinese knight-errant*. London: Routladge and Kegan Paul.

Lyman, S., and Scott, M. (1975). *Drama of social reality*. New York: Oxford University Press.

Lee, R. (1975). *A survey of Chinese herbalists*. Hong Kong: Chinese University of Hong Kong's Social Science Research Centre.

Turner, V. (1969). *The ritual process: Structure and anti-structure*. Chicago: Aldine.

Wakeman, F. (1966). *Strangers at the gate: Social disorder in south China, 1839-1861*. Berkeley, CA: University of California Press.

chapter 3

Character Formulas in Seven Stars Praying Mantis
by Dwight C. Edwards

Chinese reads: Seven Stars Praying Mantis Boxing's Twelve Character Formula. *Photos courtesy of Dwight Edwards.*

Introduction

The methodology of China's varied martial styles has been preserved in a literary heritage that has been handed down from generation to generation. At the heart of this heritage is the *zijue*, "character formula."[1] The zijue is a list of characters that is used to establish the most elemental characteristics of a particular martial style. The zijue list the style's key attributes and provides a fundamental foundation for further subdivisions of theoretical methodology.

The use of zijue is popular among many northern styles, both internal and external. The internal styles of *taijiquan* (grand ultimate fist), *baguazhang* (eight trigrams palm), and *xingyiquan* (form and mind fist) each have their own zijue.[2] Perhaps the best known of these is the thirteen postures of taijiquan.[3] *Shaolinquan* (young forest boxing), which originated in the all-important Shaolin Temple in Henan Province, is an example of an external martial art that extensively uses zijue.[4] This style is thought to have been influential to even the internal style of taijiquan, which scholars believe is due to the Chen Village's close proximity to the temple. Shaolinquan has many styles and sub-divisions that originated within the temple. Northern Praying Mantis Boxing (*Bei Tanglangquan*) is one of these styles. Its original seventeen styles are considered to be Shaolin in origin, with the eighteenth being the unifying one.[5] However, its historical development took place in Shandong Province, where it became linked to Daoism.[6]

Like so many of China's martial styles, Northern Praying Mantis is itself divided into sub-styles. These sub-styles have created a diverse number of zijue within it.[7] Having trained in Seven Stars Praying Mantis Boxing (*Qixing Tanglangquan*) for some time, I am familiar with this style's literary heritage and its various zijue. The following is an analysis of The Twelve Character Formula of Seven Star Praying Mantis Boxing.

The Arrangement of the Characters

According to tradition, the original arrangement of Seven Stars Praying Mantis Boxing's zijue is alleged to have been established four hundred years ago by its founder, Wang Lang. As with most martial styles, there is no clear evidence of this, and the great diversity of praying mantis styles makes this even more difficult to assess. However, Huang Hanxun has recorded the Seven Stars Praying Mantis literary heritage and the transmission of this style's zijue can be found in his book, *Essays on Praying Mantis Boxing* (*Tanglangquan Shu Suibi*).

Huang Hanxun, who died in 1974, was one of the most celebrated teachers in Hong Kong and possessed both scholarly and martial qualities. Many consider him to have embodied *wenwu*, "civil and martial virtues." In Hong Kong, he was known as the "Mantis King" and the inheritor of Grandmaster Luo Guangyu's Seven Stars Praying Mantis style.[8]

As outlined in *Essays on Praying Mantis Boxing*, the formula's characters are: *gou, lou, cai, gua, diao, jin* (*beng*), *diao da, zhan, nian, tie*, and *kao* (refer to list on page 47 during the following discussion). Huang's initial list is made up of eleven characters with a brief discussion of substituting *beng* with *jin*. This is the zijue transmitted within the Huang Hanxun clan and outlined below.[9]

THE TWELVE ATTRIBUTES

Gou (hook), Lou (grasp), Cai (pluck/strike)

These first three characters appearing in the formula are commonly expressed together in one fluid phrasing, *guo-lou-cai*. "Hooking" (*gou*) is initially accomplished through the unified action of intercepting, sticking, and seizing the opponent's striking arm at the wrist. Although *gou* is often translated as "hook," an analysis of the character suggest that its use has an element of "seizing." The root of this character is "hand" (the radical or root character forming the left side of this compound character), while the "hook" character is on its right.[10] "Hand" may imply that a grip using the fingers and thumb is used, as opposed to the last three fingers, which are used in another mantis style hook-hand formation called *diao*. This more active element may be inferred in all the characters that have the "hand" character as their root.

Lou (grasp) continues this character sequence and refers to grasping the opponent's arm at the elbow to facilitate control. This is classified as a trapping maneuver. This is immediately followed by *cai* (pluck), an ideogram composed of three characters. Having "hand" as its root on the left side, *cai* may indicate "plucking fruit from a tree." The compound character at the right has the character for "grasping" on top and "tree" below, indicating an action such as plucking fruit from a tree. It implies a quick jerking of the opponent's wrist in conjunction with *lou* (grasping), followed by *da* (striking).

Gou, *lou*, and *cai* are all part of a classification of techniques that Master Huang calls "the one, two, three method." Variations of this technique are demonstrated throughout the thirty-some Seven Stars Praying Mantis style handsets and are expressed in both flexible (*yin*) and firm (*yang*) methods.[11] *Gou-lou-cai* is classified as a flexible method used in the initial engagement with the opponent.

Gua (hang)

Gua, the next character in the formula's list, also has "hand" as its root. The character implies deflecting a strike upward or downward to disrupt the opponent's balance. By simultaneously striking with the rotation of the waist, this action is accomplished with the idea of body power, like many of the mantis techniques. Striking simultaneously is advantageous to any action that disrupts the opponent's equilibrium and equally promotes the tactic of "economy of motion." The use of the "hand" character in the root of *gua* suggests that gripping is involved. This action is best deployed with a trapping maneuver. Trapping is basically defined as moving the opponent's elbow across the centerline of their body. Thus this attribute also has a degree of controlling the opponent.

Diao (mantis hooking)

The next character in the formula's list is *diao*, meaning "to hook." This hand formation is the trademark of Tanglang boxing. This hand formation uses the last three fingers to hook the opponent's forearm with the thumb playing a more passive role. Unlike *gou* (hooking), which uses the thumb to grip the forearm, *diao* is not seen as a firm gripping action. This is apparent in that "hand" is not used in its ideograph. This is often a quick action that is employed in both offensive and defensive natures. The incoming strike is either rapidly deflected or the opponent's blocking arm may be snared. It is not intended as a stabilizing action, and a strike (*da*) quickly follows.

When offensive in nature, *diao* follows through with the rapid advance of a negative hook strike (a strike using the lower back wrist area), at times using the same hand to deflect and strike. If used in a defensive manner, then the strike is done with the opposite hand as the hooking hand snares the opponent's blocking forearm.

Jin (advance), Beng (recede)

In his list, Huang groups the characters *jin*, *beng*, and *da* with *diao*. *Jin* means "to advance." In martial arts practice, this is done in conjunction with a strike to facilitate an action that may confuse the opponent and often follows up with a downing tactic, such as a trap-throw. The character *jin* is an image of a "foot proceeding." Its root is "through a door." It also has the meaning of "entering." *Beng* is "to recede." This does not mean to retreat, but is the action of withdrawing to a safe distance. The ideograph is the image of a support structure, two individuals holding up a great weight; in this case a "mountain" symbolized by the character *shan*. In both cases, the idea is to use *zhan* (contact) to attach yourself to the opponent's actions, moving with them, then use the appropriate method to counter their actions. This is explained below in the attributes of *zhan* (contact) and *tie* (tag).

The idea expressed in the characters *jin* and *beng* is to "advance" and "recede" in conjunction with the shuffling footwork to play at the fringes of the opponent's striking range, while at the same time remaining within counterstriking range. This perimeter is known as "the reaction distance line."[12] This is an imaginary line between you and the opponent that is key to a successful counterattack. The safety of the reaction distance line allows you time to neutralize an opponent's action.

Da (strike)

The next character in the formula is *da*, "to strike." The opponent may initiate a strike, but the Mantis practitioner utilizes the reaction distance line and strikes first. This is accomplished through the refined utilization of body power allowing the Mantis practitioner to deflect and strike simultaneously. Huang Hanxun lists this character with *diao*, making the combination *diao da*, indicating the immediate necessity to follow the blocking maneuver with a strike. Again, the root "hand" is seen in this character.

Zhan (Contact), Nian (Cling)

The attributes thus far have dealt with the initial engagement of and bridging the distance to the opponent. The following attributes deal with close range controlling tactics.

The utilization of *zhan* (contact) and *nian* (cling) means that you must follow the opponent's action. "Contact" is to adhere to the opponent's movement from either the safety of the reaction distance line or in conjunction with "cling." "Contact/cling" implies following the opponent's advance and retreat with an appropriate response, by sticking to their every action. When bridging the opponent—that is making contact with the arm—then "clinging" is employed in conjunction with trapping tactics. Both *zhan* and *nian* have an element of stickiness, however *nian* constitutes a higher degree of sensitivity skill. *Nian* is very glutinous in nature, with a bonding force that is similar to "sticky rice," clinging to the opponent's limbs to trap and cross the elbow, while using *zhan* to adhere to their movements.

Tie (tag), Kao (lean)

Tie (tag) and *kao* (lean), the last two characters in the formula, present attributes that are utilized at close range to limit the opponent's reactions. *Tie* implies coming into contact with the opponent and *kao* implies leaning into him. With this tactic employed, the opponent's balance is disturbed. As the opponent struggles to gain equilibrium, the mantis practitioner may use a throw to bring the engagement to a conclusion. The throw is intended to injure the opponent's head or shoulder as they hit the ground.

Seven Stars Praying Mantis Boxing's Twelve Character Formula

gou	扚	lou	摟
cai	採	gua	掛
diao	刁	jin	進
beng	崩	da	打
zhan	粘	nian	黏
tie	貼	kao	靠

TECHNICAL SECTION

1) Trademark of the praying mantis style: the hookhand.

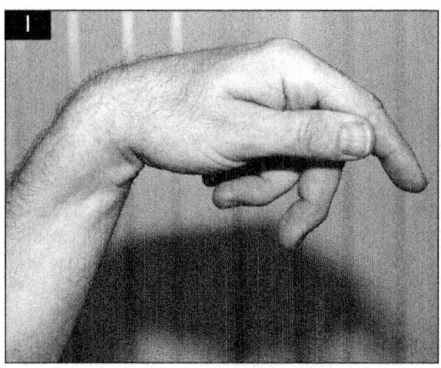

2-3) The pictures demonstrate the correct uses of the finger and thumb to grip the arm.

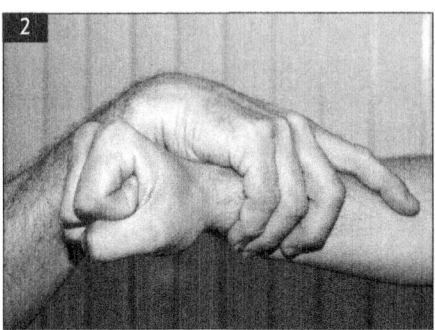
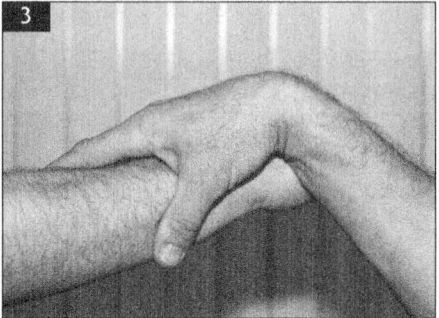

4) Demonstrating the use of *diao*, or mantis hooking.

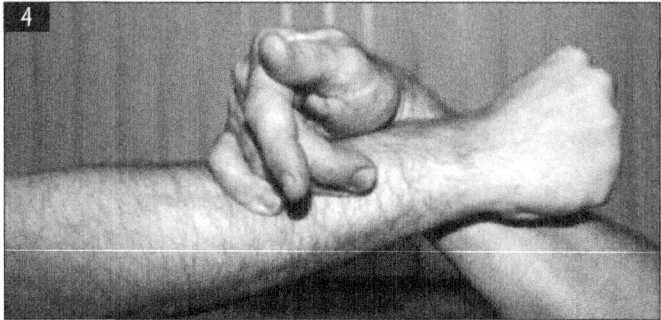

5) Here, the defender intercepts the attacker's right fist then uses a hooking grab to control the limb.

6) The defender follows by grasping the attacker's elbow to suppress the opponent's intentions by trapping his arm.
7) The grasp is immediately followed by a quick pluck, then a strike.

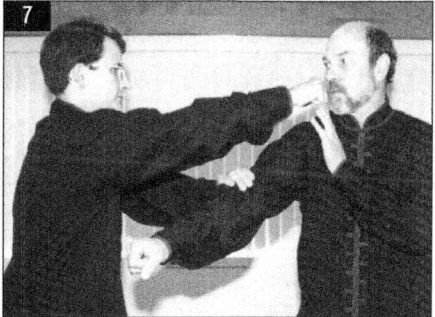

8) In a different follow-up to #5, the defender use *gua* (hang), deflecting the opponent's attack in an upward angle to open the attacker's flank to an attack.
9) In another possible follow-up to #5, using the attributes *zhan* (contact) and *nian* (cling), the defender sticks, follows and crosses the attacker's elbow.

10) The defender uses a quick flicking action of his left hand to deflect the opponent's attack in either an advancing move (*jin*) or a withdrawing move (*beng*) then (11) follows up with a strike (*da*).

As the attacker strikes forward (12), the defender steps back with his right leg and simultaneously blocks the punch by redirecting it to the side. The defender then starts to push the arm in order to gain further control. However, the attacker bridges the defender's arm and counters with a pull-trap (13). Using the attributes *tie* and *kao* (tag and hook), the attacker follows through with a waist chop palm (*qieyao zhang*) (14). By trapping and advancing, the attacker can follow the palm chop by throwing his opponent to the ground by either pressing forward or sweeping the lead leg (15).

 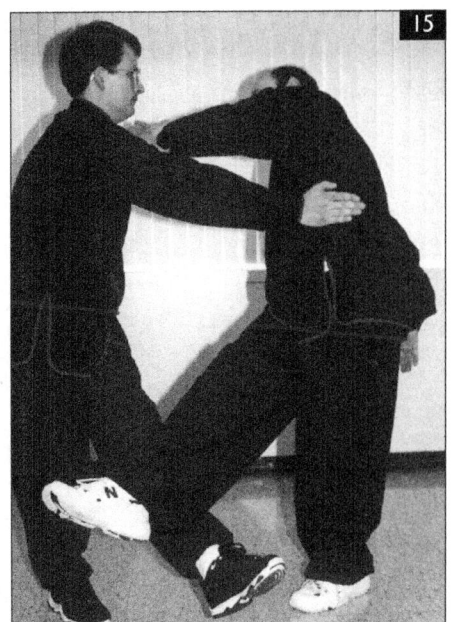

Conclusion

Although illuminating only a small portion of a style's content, the zijue is key to outlining and formulating martial systems in China. It addresses the basic attributes of a style's much broader theoretical methodologies. In Seven Stars Praying Mantis, these attributes are woven into its martial method of the Eight Rigid Methods, Twelve Flexible Methods, Eight Striking Points, Eight Non-Striking Points, Bridging Theory, Four Methods of Combat, and so on, along with the numerous phrases of application used to guide the individual throughout their practice. Through continuous re-enforcing and continued practice, these basic attributes manifest themselves in the subconscious mind. Here they become an instinctively inherent part the praying mantis practitioner's individualism, an intuitive fighting skill.

Literary heritage has been key to the preservation of China's long martial traditions. This tradition dictates that a graduate student is obligated to hand-copy his teacher's personal manuscripts, manuscripts that have been hand copied by the teacher.[13] Thanks to such contemporary teachers as Huang Hanxun, this tradition, which in ancient times was somewhat obscure, has been preserved for future generations. As Western students of Chinese martial arts thirst for their heritage, this rich literary heritage will become more apparent to the Western martial arts community.

CHARACTER TABLE

Babu Tanglangquan	Eight Step Praying Mantis Boxing	八步螳螂拳
Baguazhang	Eight Trigram Palm	八卦掌
Bei Tanglangquan (Pai)	Northern Praying Mantis Boxing (Style)	北螳螂拳（派）
Bimen Tanglangquan	Secret Door Praying Mantis Boxing	必門螳螂拳
Fan Xudong	A 4th generation praying mantis teacher	范旭東
Gejue	Formula verses	哥訣
Gongfu	Acquired skill	功夫
Huang Hanxun	A 6th generation praying mantis teacher	黃漢勛
Luo Guangyu	A 5th generation praying mantis teacher	羅光玉
Qixing Tanglangquan	Seven Star Praying Mantis Boxing	七星螳螂拳
Shaolinquan	Shaolin Temple boxing	少林拳
Shengxiao Daoren	A Daoist named Shengxiao	升霄道人
Shuaishou Tanglangquan	Brake Hand Praying Mantis Boxing	摔手螳螂拳
Taiji Tanglangquan	Grand Ultimate Praying Mantis Boxing	太極螳螂拳
Taijiquan	Grand Ultimate Boxing	太極拳
Tanglang Quanshu Suibi	*Essays on Praying Mantis Boxing*	螳螂拳書隨筆
Wenwu	Cival and martial virtues	文武
Xingyiquan	Mind-Intent Boxing	形意拳
Zijue	Character formula	字訣

FORMULA CHARACTER TABLE

ai	挨	next to (near)	*lou*	摟	grapple
bang	幫	assist	*na*	拿	seize
beng	崩	recede	*nian*	黏	cling
bi	閉	close	*nuo*	挪	remove
cai	採	pluck/strike	*qin*	擒	capture
da	打	strike	*shan*	閃	dodge
diao	刁	hooking	*shun*	順	accord with
feng	封	cover	*song*	送	accompany
gou	拘	hooking grab	*teng*	騰	move
gua	掛	hang	*ti*	提	lift
jiao	叫	shout	*tie*	貼	tag
jin	進	advance	*zhan*	粘	contact
kao	靠	lean	*zhuan*	轉	rotate
lai	來	effect (bring about)			

Notes

1. The Chinese Mandarin phonetic system used in this article is Pinyin. This is the standard form used in the People's Republic of China and literally means "to sound out." Although there are additional terms used in this tradition, such as *gejue*, I have limited this discussion to the term *zijue*.
2. Liang Shouyu and Yang Jwing-ming list the baguazhang zijue in their book *Baguazhang, Emei Baguazhang: Theory and Application*. The book gives two versions of baguazhang zijue. The first has sixteen characters and the second has twenty four. The xingyiquan's zijue can be found in their book *Hsing Yi Chuan: Theory and Application*.
3. The character formula for taijiquan is expressed in terms of *bamen* (eight gates) and *wubu* (five steps): *peng, lu, ji, an, cai, lie, zhou, guo, jinbu, tuibu, zuogu, youpan, zhongding*. An in depth discussion of taijiquan's zijue can be found in both Jou Tsung-hua's book *The Tao of T'ai Chi Ch'uan: Way to Rejuvenation* and Yang Jwing-ming's book *Advance Yang Style Tai Chi Chuan, Vol. I*.
4. Throughout the various sections in *Shaolin Wushu Daquan* are listed the corresponding *zijue, gejue*, and at times *bijue* (secret formulas) for each of the forms and techniques.
5. Tradition says that having acquired the seventeen styles of boxing, Wang Lang devised mantis boxing after long periods of observing the insect. This new insight allowed Wang to unify these styles into a reportedly greater encompassing style known as praying mantis.
6. During the Eastern Zhou Dynasty (770 B.C.E.-256 C.E.), this region was known as Qi and has a long history of Daoist culture. In Shandong, mantis boxing is associated with the Laoshan region near Qingdao city. The Seven Stars Praying Mantis Boxing tradition holds that a Daoist called Shengxiao is responsible for bringing the system out from behind the temple walls. In contrast, the Shaolin and Laoshan temples symbolize the style's attributes of hard and soft.
7. Northern Praying Mantis styles, e.g., Taiji, Beimen, Shuaishou, and Babu, are varied and each style has its own zijue (Xie and Yan, 1985: 1; Wei, 1969: 120).
8. Luo Guangyu is the fifth generation descendant in the Seven Stars Praying Mantis Boxing system. Coming from Shanghai in the 1940's, he taught at the Hong Kong branch of the Jingwu Association. Huang Hanxun was a graduate student and inheritor of the Seven Stars Praying Mantis Boxing system under Luo Guangyu.
9. As mentioned earlier, even within clan lines their exists diversity and other branches of the Luo Guangyu heritage. Many possess a variation of this list.
10. Each Chinese character has a radical within its construction. This radical

is also referred to as a root. One of three methods used to find the character's listing in a dictionary is by using the root table. The other two methods are phonetic spelling and number of strokes.

[11] Yin and yang are the basic complementary elements of Daoist philosophy. They coexist within the omnibus of Dao.

[12] This is part of the tactical theories taught to the author by his teacher Jon Funk of Vancouver, Canada, an eighth generation descendent of Huang Hanxun's clan of Seven Stars Praying Mantis.

[13] This tradition was explained to the author by his "gongfu uncle," Henry Cheng, and Henry Cheng's father, Cheng Hoyin (Huang Hanxun's graduate student from the 1950's). Fan Xudong, a fourth generation descendent, researched and compiled information on Shaolin martial methods, qigong, herbal medicine, and bone setting into the *Shaolin Authentica*. This book became part of the literary heritage of Seven Stars Praying Mantis. Cheng Hoyin said, "It took me one year to hand-copy my teacher's manuscript."

Bibliography

Dei, Q. (1995). *Shaolin wushu daquan bian shang xia* [A large collection of Shaolin martial arts, Vols. I & II]. Beijing: Beijing Sport University.

Huang, H. (1972). *Tanglang quanshu suibi* [Informal essays on praying mantis boxing]. China: Hualian Publishing.

Jou, T. (1981). *The tao of tai-chi chuan: Way to rejuvenation*. Warwick, NY: Tai Chi Foundation.

Liang, S., et al. (1996). *Baguazhang, Emei baguazhang: Theory and application*. Jamaica Plains, MA: YMAA Publication Center.

Liang, S. and Yang J. (1990). *Hsing Yi chuan: Theory and application*. Jamaica Plains, MA: YMAA Publication Center.

Tse, W. and Yan, S. (1985). *Taiji tanglang lanjie quan* [Taiji mantis volley-catch boxing]. (Chinese and English) Hong Kong: Yih Mei Book Company.

Wei, X. (1969). *Shiyong Tanglang quan* [Practical usage of praying mantis boxing]. China: Hualin Publishing.

Wieger, L. (1965). *Chinese characters: Their origin, etymology, history, classification and signification*. New York: Dover Publications.

Yang, J. and Bolt, J. (1981). *Shaolin Long Fist kung fu*. Hollywood, CA: Unique Publication.

Zhao, F. (1989, October). Tanglang quan shoufa gang mu shishi [A general outline examining the hand methods of praying mantis boxing]. *Zhonghua wushu* [Chinese Martial Arts], 24.

Acknowledgment: A special thanks to my students Brian Schmidgall and Joe Groesch who appear in the technical section.

chapter 4

The Traditional History of
Plum Blossom Praying Mantis Boxing
by Ilya Profatilov, M.A.

Wang Lang, the founder of praying mantis boxing.
All illustrations courtesy of I. Profatilov.

Introduction

The origins of praying mantis boxing (*tanglang quan*) are obscure. The main obstacle for the researcher is the lack of written records and historical artifacts. The only relatively reliable historical information comes from old manuscripts that describe the origins, theory, and curriculum of praying mantis boxing. There is also a vast array of oral folk traditions, legends, fantastic stories, and songs that can be used as a source for outlining the style's basic history and to add color to the picture.

Traditionally, praying mantis boxing is believed to have existed for over one thousand years. It has grown into numerous schools and branches. As related by the older generation of praying mantis boxing masters, the early style was called simply *tanglang quan*. The name "Plum Blossom Praying Mantis Boxing" emerged in the late 19th century to distinguish the original style from later deviations. Praying mantis belongs to the group of so-called "hard" styles and, with its "cousin" Seven Stars Praying Mantis Boxing, which Wang Yongchun (1854-1926) developed in the late 1880's, forms an opposition to the only "soft" praying mantis style, Six Harmonies Praying Mantis Boxing.

There are three major Plum Blossom Praying Mantis Boxing branches: Jiang Hualong's, Hao Lianru's, and Sun Yuanchang's. Although they share the same roots and theory, the techniques, forms, and applications occasionally vary from branch to branch. Often the three are referred to by the same names, which can be confusing.

Jiang Hualong's (1855-1924) branch is usually called Plum Blossom Praying Mantis Boxing. In Taiwan, this style of boxing is mistakenly called Seven Stars Praying Mantis. The most famous contemporary masters of this branch were the "Three Mountains of Laiyang City" (*Laiyang de San Shan*): Wang Yushan (1892-1976), Cui Shoushan (1890-1969), and Li Kunshan (1894-1976). Today the most renowned grandmaster of this school is Wang's son, Wang Yuanqian (b. 1934).

Left: Master Wang Yuanqian and the author.
Right: Historical weapons in the Shaolin Monastery.

Hao Lianru's (1864-1904) branch is generally known as Hao Family Plum Blossom Praying Mantis. The most prominent contemporary masters of this style were Hao Henglu (1887-1945/52), Cao Dekun (c.1885-1959), Hao Bin (1900-1984), and Chen Yuntao (1906-1978). The most renowned grandmaster of this school in modern times was Ma Hanqing (1920-1997).

Sun Yuanchang's branch is known as Grand Ultimate Praying Mantis or Grand Ultimate Plum Blossom Praying Mantis. This branch eventually split into two main schools, the Yantai school in Shandong and the Hong Kong school. The most well-known contemporary masters of the Yantai school were Ren Fengrui, Chi Shoujin, Su Kebin, and Wang Guodian. The Hong Kong school, which is the better known of the two, was founded by Zhao Zhuxi (1900-1991; Chiu Chuk-kai in Cantonese).

The Development of Praying Mantis Boxing[1]

The founder of praying mantis boxing was Wang Lang, who lived during the Northern Song Dynasty era (969-1126). Tradition says that Wang Lang participated in a tournament, where in he fought with many masters, in the capital of Kaifeng near the famous Shaolin Monastery. When Han Tong defeated Wang Lang, Wang left the city full of bitterness. At one point along the road, he rested under a tree. Wang suddenly noticed a praying mantis in the middle of the wheel tracks in the road. The praying mantis lifted its front legs, which resembled broad swords, and looked directly up at an approaching chariot. Wang Lang laughed at the tiny insect that did not know its own limitations in size and strength. He picked up the praying mantis and threw it away from the path. However, the insect returned to its place in front of the approaching chariot, attacked the wheel with his sharp knife-like front hooks, and then ducked to avoid the chariot and flew away unharmed.

Wang Lang had a sudden enlightenment. After his return home, he carefully observed the agile and skillful techniques of a praying mantis trying to catch its prey. Wang developed fighting techniques based on his observations, creating a new style. After several years of practice, during which he perfected the new techniques, Wang Lang finally defeated Han Tong in a fight. It is said that Song Dynasty Emperor Zhao Kuangyin (927-976) admired Wang Lang's technique so much that he invited him to be a general in his court. Wang declined the invitation. Thus began the new style, praying mantis boxing.

At approximately the same time, Chan Buddhist Master Fu Ju became abbot of the Shaolin Temple. Driven by a desire to improve the Shaolin martial arts, Fu Ju invited eighteen boxing masters to teach at the temple. Among them was Wang Lang. Wang later incorporated the most essential techniques of the seventeen other masters into praying mantis.

In the *Praying Mantis Boxing Manual* (1794), the unknown author[2] provides a list of the masters whom Abbot Fu invited to the monastery, as well as their boxing styles:

1) In the beginning, there was Emperor Tai Zu's Long-Range Boxing [*changquan*].
2) Master Han Tong's Through the Back [*tongbei*] Boxing is considered parental.
3) Master Zhang En's hand technique "wrap around and seal" [*chan feng*] is especially profound.
4) Master Ma Ji's Close-Range Strikes [*duanda*] Boxing is the most remarkable.
5) It is impossible to come close to Master Huang You, who knows

close-range hand techniques [*kao shou*].
6) Master Jin Xiang's "blocking hands and following through fist" [*keshou tongquan*] technique.
7) Master Liu Xing's "hooking, scooping, and grabbing hands" [*gou lou cai shou*] techniques.
8) Master Yan Qing's "sticking, grabbing, and falling" [*zhanna diefa*] techniques.
9) Master Wen Yuan's Short Boxing [*duanquan*] is most extraordinary.
10) Master Sun Heng's Monkey Boxing [*houquan*] is also impressive.
11) Master Mien Shen's Cotton Fist [*mianquan*] is lightning fast.
12) Master Huai De's "throwing-grabbing and hard crashing" [*shuailue yingbeng*] techniques.
13) Master Tan Fang's technique of "ducking, leaping, and passing through the ears" [*gunlou guaner*].
14) Master Lin Chong's "mandarin duck" [*yuanyang jiao*] kick is the strongest kicking technique.
15) Master Meng Su's "seven postures of continuous fist strikes" [*qishi lanquan*] techniques.
16) Master Yang Gun's "hand binding and grabbing" [*kunlu zhenru*] techniques instantly attack.
17) Master Cui Lian's "explosive strikes into the hollow parts of the body" [*woli paochui*] techniques.
18) Master Wang Lang's Praying Mantis Boxing absorbed and equalized all previous techniques.

A Shaolin Monastery book has the same list in a slightly different order and concludes with, "All these were gathered and brought together by Chan Master Fu Ju from Shaolin Monastery" (De, 1988: 5).

Eventually, Fu Ju organized Wang Lang's praying mantis techniques into boxing manuals. At that time, praying mantis boxing was called "Secret Hands." All materials of the praying mantis boxing that Fu Ju collected were passed on to the Daoist priest Shengxiao Daoren. Further transmissions are unknown and there are no additional records of the style until three hundred years later. Praying mantis boxing then reappears during Emperor Qianlong's reign (1736-1796) during the Qing Dynasty.

The First and Second Generations: Li Bingxiao and the Nameless Outlaw

Li Bingxiao was born in Fujian Province in south China during the 17th century. When his father received an official position in Shandong Province, Bingxiao followed him, moving to an area near Laiyang and Haiyang cities.

The *Laiyang County Gazetteer* records:

> Praying mantis boxing was transmitted numerous times, approaching perfection with each passing day. After some time, a man from Xiao Chishan Village in Laiyang County, Li Bingxiao, assumed the role of praying mantis' First Patriarch.

However, a boxing manual written by praying mantis Master Cui Shoushan states:

> When the Qing Dynasty [1664-1911] Manchus organized the public offices of their regime, they began selecting government officials through tests of both military and literary ability. Thereafter, the martial arts were slowly revived. At that time, a candidate for the civil service from Haiyang County named Li Bingxiao was preparing for the literary examination. He competed in the fall examination but failed. Thereafter, his wordly desires abated and he went into seclusion. His greatest pleasure then lay in meeting with passing travelers. He met many different chevaliers and wandering knights [*xiake*]. Thus Li Bingxiao learned equally well the best of both the internal and external boxing schools. He came only to practice the art of praying mantis boxing and thereby mastered the style's quintessence. Thereafter, he chose to lead the life of a vagabond, not revealing his name to anyone he encountered. It is for this reason that almost no one knows of him today.

View of the main street of the modern Chishan Village.

Similar information was provided by Zhao Mingde, a 73-year-old resident of modern Chishan Village and a sixth generation descendant of

Li Bingxiao's only disciple, Zhao Zhu. According to Mingde, Li was from neighboring Haiyang County. The *Laiyang County Gazetteer* contains somewhat different information on the origins of Li Bingxiao's teachings:

> During the Qian Long reign [1736-1796], Li Bingxiao followed his father on a tour of official duty to southern China. At that time, there was a prodigious outlaw in the south who had been captured and put in prison. While in prison, the outlaw became so ill that he lost consciousness and was unable to recognize others. The prison warden reported this to a government official, who ordered the outlaw released. Li Bingxiao considered the circumstances and reflected upon the principles of medicine. He examined the bandit's bodily palpitations, purchased medicine, and had the bandit drink it. The bandit then broke into a sweat and eventually regained consciousness. Later, the outlaw waited for an opportunity and escaped surreptitiously in the middle of the night.
>
> Late one night several months later, Li Bingxiao was sitting alone when the bandit knocked at his window. The bandit thanked Li for healing him. Li Bingxiao was overjoyed to speak with the bandit. The bandit taught his art of praying mantis boxing to Li Bingxiao who, being talented and athletic, mastered the new skills. After that, the bandit never returned.
>
> Soon, Li Bingxiao became known as "Two Hooks" [ergou] Li and sometimes was called "Old Man With Two Hooks" for his unique manner of applying certain praying mantis hooking techniques. When Li Bingxiao returned home, praying mantis boxing became increasingly rooted in Laiyang. To date, it has been handed down for eight generations and no practitioner throughout those generations taught the system to outsiders. Therefore, what people call Great Ultimate Praying Mantis Boxing or, alternatively, Plum Blossom Praying Mantis Boxing, in all cases refer to this system.

Master Li Bingxiao taught only one disciple—Zhao Zhu.

The Third Generation: Zhao Zhu

Zhao Zhu, also known as Zhao Qilu, was from Da Chishan Village, which shares a border with Xiao Chishan Village.[3] As a young man, Zhao Zhu heard about his famous neighbor Li Bingxiao and kowtowed to him to learn praying mantis boxing, becoming Li Bingxiao's only disciple. Eventually, Zhao Zhu completed his training and became the system's third-generation inheritor. Unfortunately, there are almost no data regarding Zhao's life. The only historical information is derived from the *Zhao Family Genealogical Records*, which prove he was a real figure. Another reliable source, the *Laiyang County Gazetteer*, reports one short story about Zhao Zhu:

Once when Zhu was an old man, he was sitting cross-legged on top of his bed when a notorious bandit, Wei San, suddenly entered the room and attacked Zhu, attempting to gouge out his eyes. With a wave of his hand, Zhu threw Wei San under his bed. The bandit was so shocked that he did not dare make even the slightest movement.

There is another story regarding Zhao Zhu:

After many years of diligent training, Zhao Zhu inherited Li Bingxiao's complete teachings. The time came for the aged Master Li to return to his home village to celebrate Chinese New Year. Zhao Zhu walked him to the river that lay on their way. Li Bingxiao stopped before the river and said, "I have already taught you all my boxing techniques. However, there is still one skill left. It is called 'Swallow Crossing the River.' Next year, I will teach you upon my return." Zhao Zhu listened and invited his teacher to step onto the ferry, but Li Bingxiao leaped into the air, landing on the thin ice that partly covered the river, and effortlessly walked to the opposite bank. Zhao Zhu stood in amazement. That was a demonstration of the art of "weightless body skills." Unfortunately, Li Bingxiao never returned. He passed away that year in his village and thus the "weightless body skills" became a lost art of praying mantis boxing.
– Wang Yuanqian interviews

These two stories illustrate Zhao Zhu's fame and martial skills. Tradition states that Zhao Zhu passed on his art only to his disciple Liang Xuexiang. Nonetheless, the latest research reveals that Zhao Zhu also taught his son. Thus a fifth-generation descendant of Zhao Zhu, the late Zhao Qingzhi, was the last representative of this direct family transmission.

Representatives of the sixth and seventh generations of direct descendants of Zhao Zhu's family: Zhao Mingde and Zhao Yongshou.

The Fourth Generation: Liang Xuexiang

Liang Xuexiang (1810-?; aka Liang Shupu) was born in Yushan Kuang Village, almost two and a half miles southeast of Da Chishan Village, which is on the border between Haiyang and Laiyang Counties in Shandong. As a young man, Liang became Zhao Zhu's disciple and quickly mastered praying mantis boxing. It is said that he used to practice boxing routines under an "Eight Immortals Table"—an octagonal table used to train strength, precision, and endurance. Liang Xuexiang was a man of medium stature but remarkably agile. His striking power was also extraordinary. He once killed a challenger with one punch; people therefore called him "Iron Fist" Liang. Nevertheless, his physical strength was below ordinary. Because he could not even lift a heavy basket of grain, his father frequently criticized him for being unproductive during the daily agricultural labor.

Liang spent the first half of his adult life working as a bodyguard for a protection bureau. He also traveled around China seeking out other boxing masters. It is told that he taught boxing in Beijing and was even promoted to the rank of seventh-degree official after passing the government military exams.[4] After his retirement from the capital at the age of 45, Liang again became a bodyguard for rich landlords in the Laiyang area. On one occasion, 36 armed bandits from Shanxi Province came to extort money from one of the landlords in Laiyang City and to kill Liang, for whom they had been hunting for a long time. Master Liang alone defeated all 36 bandits but lost an eye in the battle. Thereafter, his nickname was "One Eyed" Liang.

Another version of this story states that Liang once was escorting a caravan of silver. It stopped for the night at a small inn in an area near Cangzhou that was controlled by bandits. That night, over thirty heavily armed bandits attacked the inn. Liang grabbed a pole and fearlessly fought the bandits. In the middle of the fight, his pole was cut into pieces, but Liang continued fighting and ultimately defeated the intruders with his bare hands. The caravan left Cangzhou to avoid more trouble. Unfortunately, during the fight Liang's braid, which he had wrapped around his head as was the custom at that time, slid onto his face and covered one eye. The constant rubbing and scouring of the hair irritated his eye, which became infected. This infection eventually led to the loss of the eye.

Soon after this battle, Liang retired from protection services and committed himself to propagating praying mantis boxing. Liang's fame as a boxer was widespread in the Shandong peninsula and many people wanted to learn from him. Liang returned to his home village, Yushan Kuang, Haiyang County, where he remained for the rest of his life, teaching and promoting praying mantis boxing, combining it with an extensive practice of traditional Chinese medicine.

Yushan Kuang Village.

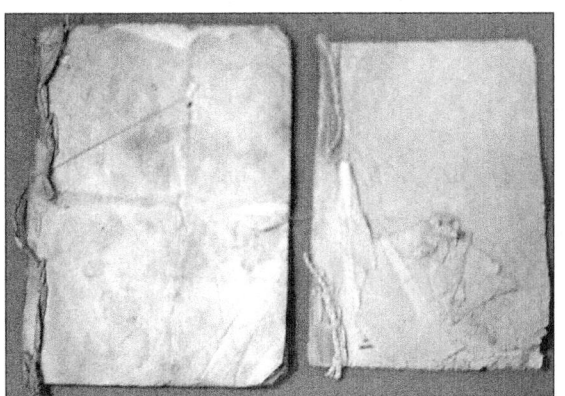 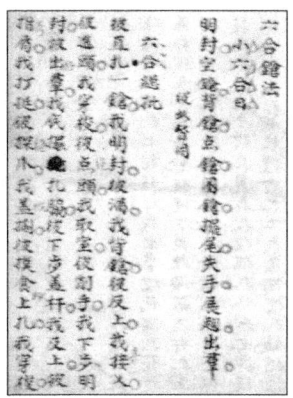

The original handwritten manuscript of
the *Long Spear Manual* by Liang Xuexiang
preserved by the Liang family.

During this time, Liang Xuexiang developed praying mantis boxing theory and authored at least three boxing manuals. The first was composed during the Xianfeng reign (1851-1862) and was entitled *Boxing, Staff and Spear Fencing Manual*. It contained essential theory and the names of the three original praying mantis forms: "Crash and Fill In," "Chaotically Connected" (also known as "Plum Blossom"), and "Separating the Body Into Eight Elbows." The second manual, *Boxing Manual*, was written in 1853. The third was *Long Spear Manual*.

The original *Long Spear Manual* was preserved by the Liang family and was unknown in the praying mantis boxing community until the winter of 1999, when Liang Zhengzhao and Liang Fengzhong (fifth- and sixth-generation direct descendants of Liang Xuexiang, respectively) gave it to Wang Yuanqian.

Liang Xuexiang was the first praying mantis boxing master to break from the tradition of passing the art to only one disciple. He eventually passed his art to his son, Liang Jingchuan, Jiang Hualong, Song Zide, Hao Hong (Lianru), Xiu Shankun, Sun Ying, Zhu Yongxiu, Jiang Laoqi, Tong Kunjiang, Sun Yuanchang, and Sun Yuancai. Among these, Jiang Hualong became the most famous.

Legend says that, one day, aged Master Liang practiced the form "Chaotically Connected," went into his house, quietly sat down, closed his eyes, and passed away.

The Fifth Generation: Jiang Hualong and Song Zide

Jiang Hualong (1855-1924; aka Yunsheng) was born to a poor family during the fifth year of the Xianfeng reign (1851-1862) in Huangjin Gou Village, Laiyang County, Shandong Province. Song Zide (1855-1933/34; aka Yaokun) was born to a wealthy family in Zhaoge Zhuang Village, Laiyang County. He was also called "Second Elder" Song.

Left: Taiji Tanglang Quan Grandmaster Song Zide (1855-1933/34).
Right: Representatives of the fifth and sixth generations
of direct descendants of Liang Xuexiang's family:
Mr. Liang Zhengzhao and Mr. Liang Fengzhong.

Since childhood, Jiang and Song were close friends and boxing brothers. They learned monkey boxing prior to their introduction to praying mantis boxing with Master Liang Xuexiang. When the two started training in Liang's boxing school, Jiang, although he was extremely talented, was not diligent enough and arrogantly bragged about his boxing skills. So Liang decided to teach him a lesson. He wrote a letter to his first disciple and ordered him to punish young Jiang. Jiang was chosen to personally deliver that letter. As soon as Liang's disciple read the letter he charged at Jiang and gave him a sound beating. Young Jiang left in tears and went to tell Liang what happened. Liang replied, "Look at yourself! You are such a great boxing master! How come you could not win the fight?" Jiang Hualong then trained diligently and behaved humbly.

Eventually, Jiang and Song became disciples of Liang Xuexiang, but he would only teach them one praying mantis form. This was because of the old conservative mentality that allowed the transmission of the style to only one meritorious disciple. Liang taught them "Eight Elbows," an archaic form of close-range fighting that has been traced to Wang Lang. Liang had his own reason for teaching this form to his students. He knew that the "Eight Elbows" form, although it was a very effective set of techniques, could not be used successfully without the complimentary techniques taught in the remaining praying mantis "Secret Hands" forms: "Crash and Fill In," "Chaotically Connected," and six sections of "Essentials." Liang wanted to find the most dedicated and faithful disciples before he transmitted the entire system.

After Song and Jiang completed their training with Liang, Jiang was challenged by a famous fighter from Laiyang named Ji, who was a military official. Even with Jiang's good fighting skills, he was defeated. Ashamed and frustrated, Jiang went to his friend Song and told him about his failure. Song came up with a plan to persuade Master Liang to teach them the core of the praying mantis system, the set of six forms called "Essentials," and the rest of the forms. Song told Jiang to go to Master Liang's house and kneel in front of the gates until Liang agreed to teach the entire system. Song also told Jiang to tell Master Liang that they would take a vow to take care of him for the rest of his life and that Song would even provide the finances to build a house for him. So Jiang did as Song suggested. After a day of kneeling in front of Liang's gates, he was finally brought into the house by Liang, who asked the reason for the kneeling, affectionately calling Jiang by his childhood name "Mountain" (*Shan*). After a great deal of persuasion, Liang agreed to teach Jiang the complete system.

When Jiang returned to Song's home, the two young men knelt in front of the altar and took a vow to be sworn brothers. From then on, Song would call Jiang "2nd Brother" and, according to Jiang and Song's agreement, Jiang taught all Liang Xuexiang's forms and techniques to Song as he learned them from Liang. Afterward, the two men trained together, perfecting their skills.

Song built a six-room house for Liang, where Jiang and Song would later open a boxing school and give all the money they earned to Liang. The new house was built behind the Liang family house in Yushan Kuang Village, Haiyang County. Both houses still exist. A sixth-generation descendant of Liang Xuexiang, Liang Zhengzhao, a local physician of traditional Chinese medicine, lives in the old Liang family house and his son, Liang Fengzhong, lives in three rooms of the house built by Song and Jiang. The other three rooms are sealed and remain uninhabited.

There is a story that once, during the training of a praying mantis "hard qigong" technique called "Three Returns and Nine Rotations of Buddhist Arhats," Song and Jiang's students destroyed a wall inside the house while conditioning their bodies by striking them continuously against the wall. This story grew into a legend with a slightly different version:

> After the house was completed, Jiang Hualong accompanied Master Liang to look at the new house. "This is a very lovely house," Liang said, "but it doesn't seem to be very strong. It will not be able to resist if I hit it with a hip-elbow smash." As soon as he had said this, Liang hit the side of the house with a hip-elbow smash. Just as he had predicted, the wall fell to pieces. Master Liang Xuexiang was that powerful.

Left: Entrance into Liang Xuexiang's original house in Yushan Kuang Village.
Right: Master Liang Xuexiang's "new" house, which was also his boxing school.

After a few years (traditionally in praying mantis boxing, only one form was taught each year), both Jiang and Song became proficient in praying mantis. Song even surpassed Jiang. One day, they were sitting and drinking tea. Song pulled out a tobacco pipe and asked Jiang to light it. Jiang, while lighting the pipe, struck Song in the rib cage with a punch but immediately found himself on the floor, thrown by Song's lighting-fast counter. When Jiang stood up, he bowed to Song and said that Song's martial skills surpassed his own.

Except for the often obscure boxing compilations by the Daoist priest Shengxiao Daoren, which were based on the original Song Dynasty materials of Shaolin Abbot Fu Ju, there were no written sources or complete manuals on praying mantis boxing. Liang Xuexiang was the first person to compile a basic comprehensive manual on the style. He gave all of his writings to Jiang Hualong. These contained essential theory and the names of some forms.

Unfortunately, Jiang was illiterate so he gave these pages to Song Zide and asked him to develop a new, comprehensive manual. During the Tong Zhi reign (1862-1875), after a few years of hard work, Song Zide, with the help of Jiang, wrote a new 162-page manual containing information on praying mantis boxing's theory, history, forms, weapons, and qigong. In the early 1980's, Song's grandson, Wang Yuanqian, donated the original copy to the Beijing Wushu Association (*Beijing Shi Wushu Xiehui*).

Master Wang Yuanqian with the Tanglang Quan "Boxing Manual" written by his grandfather, Song Zide.

According to Wang Yuanqian:

> Jiang Hualong had an extremely difficult personality. Whenever he was offended by someone, he would challenge that person and defeat him. When Jiang Hualong was in bad spirits, he would walk the streets looking like a raging bull and it was not a good time to be in his way.

At the end of the Qing Dynasty, when Jiang Hualong was living and teaching in the Yantai area, he would often challenge or be challenged by masters of other boxing styles. He defeated them all. As a result, a number of frustrated boxers who had lost to Jiang got together. Eight Trigrams Boxing (*baguaquan*) Master Gong Baotian (1867-1943), whom Jiang had recently defeated, acted as a representative of these Yantai boxing masters and challenged Jiang. He invited Jiang to Shinanhu, Yantai, to fight them with weapons to the death.

When Jiang heard the news, he burst with anger and rushed back to his native Laiyang County. He took his swords and long spear and put on helmet and armor as if he were going to war. His disciples followed him. Jiang jumped on a horse and was about to gallop off when he was stopped by his friend and boxing brother, Song Zide. Song told him that this was not an honorable thing to do and that, in the long run, this incident would cause even more trouble.

Eventually, Song talked Jiang out of going and Song instead went to Yantai to settle the matter. In Yantai, he met Gong Baotian, who was reasonable enough to recognize all of the possible unpleasant consequences that could be the aftermath of this conflict. Thus Song restored the peace between the Yantai martial arts community and Jiang Hualong. Later, Jiang was invited to teach praying mantis in Yantai, where he stayed for a few months until the tragic death of his only son, Jiang Huanting, who was one of the few who truly perfected praying mantis boxing. He often traveled with his father and helped him teach. He died at a young age because of heart problems. Jiang was sixty years old at the time. Eventually, Song Zide's servant offered his daughter to Jiang Hualong as a wife. Jiang accepted, but the couple did not bear any male children. Therefore, Jiang Hualong adopted a son whom he called Jiang Huanzhi and to whom he taught praying mantis boxing.

Jiang Hualong became extremely famous. Popular sayings referred to him as "Master of kicking and punching is Jiang Hualong, and master of broadsword and spear is Li Yongde"[5] and "Jiang Hualong is a ferocious fighter and Li Mingge is a spiteful fighter." Thus, according to popular belief, only Li Mingge's skills were equal to Jiang's.

Li Mingge (1858-1913), who took as his second name Zhongxiang, was from Gezhuang Village. Later, Li became better known under the soubriquet

Danbai. Li Danbai was a master of Long-Range Boxing, Yan Qing's Boxing, and Three Coordination Skills, a ground fighting boxing style.[6] He was well known in martial arts circles as "One who does not have enemies in the empire under Heaven."

According to the *Laiyang County Gazetteer*, Li Danbai had an imposing physical bearing that surpassed that of any other. He began his training under Long-Range Boxing Master Gao Dianji, and also studied under Yu Zhixiu. Yu was a practitioner of Iron Legs ground boxing and hailed from Xiaoli Village. His system was a mixture of the most hard-earned tactics from the various schools of boxing. Regardless of all these boxing systems, Li Danbai had his favorite empty-hand form called the Main Set of Turning a Water Wheel. He spent all of his time perfecting this form and brought it to new heights while developing extraordinary fighting skills.

Li Danbai served as a rear guard in Jiang Zhenlian's Northern Qixia troops, who guarded the county against attacks by Nian bandits.[7] Jiang Zhenlian was said to condition his body to a considerable degree by, among other methods, sleeping every night on a brick pillow. He was also widely known for his leg techniques.

Later, Li Danbai took an official appointment as a bodyguard for the Xinjiang Province military governor. After many years of service, Li heard about Jiang Hualong, who had opened a boxing school in Laiyang County. Li had also heard from his teacher, Yu Zhixi, who was reputed to have said, "I have competed against I don't know how many hundreds or thousands of men from seven provinces. Of all these, there are only two whom I respect as equals" (*Laiyang County Gazeteer*, c. 1935: 1050). The two men to whom he was referring were a Mr. Zheng from Shanxi and Jiang Hualong.

Li Danbai also heard that Jiang Hualong claimed that no one in China could compare with him in martial arts skills. In 1908, Li Danbai decided to return to Laiyang and meet Jiang Hualong in a fight. Jiang, who was teaching in Yantai, heard about Li Danbai's intentions and decided to go back to Laiyang to meet Li. The two masters met at the boxing school of Master Liu Mingchang.

After an introductory dinner, both masters were ready to fight. Jiang, as described in the *Laiyang County Gazetteer*, "was not even five-feet tall and looked as fat and dull as a village imbecile, but when his skills were tested, he was as nimble and dexterous as a monkey." On the contrary, Li Danbai "was a huge man standing almost six-feet and had enormous strength." Wang Yuanqian describes the fight as follows:

> The fight was fast. Li Danbai attacked first with the continuous strikes of his favorite technique, Six Hands of Turning a Water Wheel, and forced Jiang

Hualong to retreat until at last he was up against the wall. Nevertheless, Jiang Hualong used a technique called Suspended Strikes to the Left and Right, and pushed Li Danbai to the opposite wall. Then the two masters were stopped by Liu Mingchang who already understood that both men were equal in strength and skill.

Eventually the three famous boxers—Jiang Hualong, Li Danbai, and Song Zide—became sworn brothers. Li Danbai was the elder brother, Jiang Hualong was the second, and Song Zide was the third.

The *Laiyang County Gazetteer* noted:

> From that time on, both masters greatly respected each other and became sworn brothers. Because Danbai and Hualong were close friends, the disciples of their two schools mutually benefited from the teachings of both masters. The one man who received Li Danbai's full teachings was Xu Zhizhuo of Shihe Village.

Li's Main Set of Turning a Water Wheel form so impressed Jiang Hualong that he incorporated it into the praying mantis boxing system with some modifications. Later, while living in Yantai, Jiang taught the Main Set of Turning a Water Wheel to many praying mantis masters and the form became known simply as Turning a Water Wheel. Eventually, this form developed into the Major Turning a Water Wheel and Minor Turning a Water Wheel forms.

Master Wang Yuanqian demonstrates
long spear fighting techniques.

Master Wang Yuanqian and the author
demonstrate long spear fighting techniques.

Unfortunately, Li Danbai became seriously ill when he was 55-years-old. Before his death, Li told his 17-year-old nephew, Li Kunshan, "I searched throughout all China and the best boxing master I have ever seen is your named uncle Jiang Hualong. When I leave this world, you should become his disciple. If you study the skill of boxing diligently, you will have great success" (Li, HJ interview; Li, HJ, 1992: 17).

The praying mantis boxing system that Jiang Hualong and Song Zide taught had only three classical weapons: Purple-Golden Staff of the Great One,[8] Jade Ring Broadsword of the Great Ultimate, and Jade Ring Double-Handed Straight Sword. Jiang had basic Six Harmonies Long Spear training skills, which he learned from Liang Xuexian. However, Jiang felt that the style lacked the fourth classical Chinese weapon, the spear, which is considered to be "the king of weapons." Jiang Hualong heard about a famous long spear master from Laiyang, "Old Man" Wang Taichu. He was known for his reluctance to teach his advanced spear techniques.

Jiang went to "Old Man" Wang and challenged him to fight with spears in the courtyard. Wang parried Jiang's thrust and counterattacked with a thrust at Jiang's throat. Jiang found himself in a poor situation and retreated as fast as he could. When Jiang hit the opposite wall, the tip of Wang's spear was still pressed firmly but well controlled at Jiang's thorax. Astonished, Jiang Hualong declared himself defeated. Ashamed, he left Wang's house.

Jiang went to Song Zide and told him the story. Song was shocked by Jiang's disrespectful behavior. "Old Man" Wang was much more advanced in years than Jiang and was a well-respected master. Song insisted that Jiang

Hualong go and apologize for his rude behavior. Jiang did so and was forgiven by Wang Taichu.

Eventually, Jiang Hualong and Song Zide asked Wang to teach them. Wang agreed only because Jiang was famous for his bare-hand combat skills and Wang, who was a quite ordinary boxer, wanted to exchange his experience with Jiang. Jiang and Song trained with Wang for several years, spending the first three years refining the three basic techniques of the long spear: sealing, pressing, and thrusting (or outside circular block, inside circular block, and thrust).

After three years, they could unbutton each others' cotton buttons with the tip of a 10.8-foot spear and lift eyelids and upper lip with a spear tip without causing any harm to the person. They also could thrust a spear tip into an opponents' chin and leave a deep red spot but no trace of blood. Thus the praying mantis boxing long spear techniques taught by Jiang and Song bear a strong resemblance to Wang Taichu's.

Song and Jiang are also credited with developing the open-hand form called Plum Blossom Path, which was later adopted by other praying mantis styles. Song created the seventh form of the Essentials set as a combination of praying mantis boxing and ground boxing. The seventh form is one of the rarest forms and was taught only by Song Zide's grandson, Wang Yuanqian.

Many accomplished martial artists traveled to Laiyang to learn from Song Zide. Among them were some who challenged Song and were defeated. One of these boxing masters came to test Song when he was in the process of healing a man from pain by using a praying mantis boxing qigong form, the Three Returns and Nine Rotations Method of Arhats. Song was not wearing his shoes, which he had placed near the doorway. When the challenger entered the room, the first thing he saw was the large shoes. His imagination drew an immediate picture of his defeat by a big man, the owner of the shoes. The challenger turned around and left quickly. That is how Song's fame defeated a man without fighting.

When Jiang Hualong and Song Zide were middle-aged, they decided to teach openly and together established a boxing school in Zhaoge Zhuang Village, Laiyang County. At that time, Jiang did not like to teach. He often just observed or supervised the training while Song did most of the teaching. When Jiang was 60 years old, he decided to start teaching on his own and opened a second school in Chang Shan Village, Laiyang. However, he would often visit the Zhaoge Zhuang school and help Song teach.

When Jiang started teaching in the Chang Shan school, he altered the Grand Ultimate Praying Mantis Boxing that he used to teach in his Zhaoge Zhuang school with Song. He both modified and omitted some original forms. For instance, because of relative similarities in the techniques, Jiang did not teach the Crash and Fill In form to his students who had already learned the Plum Blossom Path form and vice versa. Jiang made changes to the Essentials set, which later led to the creation of a slightly modified set of six Essentials. Jiang taught this new version of praying mantis only to his students at the Chang Shan school.

Modern Chang Shan Village.

Around 1912, while in Yantai, Jiang developed a close relationship with two boxing experts, Chen Deshan and Wang Zhongqing, from whom he learned the best techniques of Long-Range Boxing, Connected-Arms Boxing, Eight-Trigrams Boxing, and Form-Mind Boxing (xingyiquan). Eventually, Jiang Hualong's experiments with different styles of martial arts led to the creation of a new praying mantis style. He became the initiator and cofounder of a combination style based on these systems' techniques, which were fused to create an entirely different set of Essentials. This set of six forms became the core of the new boxing system, "Six Harmonies Boxing" or "Harmonious Righteousness Boxing," perhaps in honor of the Boxer Rebellion (1898-1900).

Song Zide disapproved of Jiang's innovation, firmly stating that they should teach the traditional system and that they should not create a new style. Nevertheless, Jiang believed in his innovations and taught a few people this new style. Among those to learn was a Daoist priest, Feng Huanyi (1879-?), who passed on the style, as Eight Steps Praying Mantis, to Wei Xiaotang (1901-1984).

As mentioned earlier, Jiang Hualong was not a tall man, standing only five feet, two inches, but he had an incredible physique and was built like a solid column of muscle. Such a rock-hard body and great physical strength were a result of praying mantis "hard qigong" body conditioning. This hard qigong consisted of exercises such as The Method of the Fourteen Exercises of the Six Ground Immortals, the Eight Pieces of Brocade Method of Body Conditioning of the Daoist Taiyi, and the Three Returns and Nine Rotations Method of Arhats.

There are many stories about Jiang Hualong's great qigong skills. It was said that when Jiang was in a deep sleep, a stone thrown at him would not harm him because the "protective" qi would naturally concentrate in the area affected by the blow and prevent damage. Another story told that Jiang could lie on the ground and have a person drop a large grinding stone on his stomach and the stone would bounce off half a yard. Jiang also used to sleep standing on his head, with his feet sticking straight up in the air, in a stone mortar that was used for husking rice. This was part of his daily qigong training.

Jiang Hualong and Song Zide were the most important figures in the development of praying mantis boxing at the turn of the 20th century. Together they trained eight of the most famous disciples of this lineage, who were known as the Eight Great Disciples: Wang Yushan, Cui Shoushan, Li Kunshan, Jiang Huanting, Zhao Shiting, Jiu Zhuyuan, Zang Yunsheng, and Jiang Yulong. Most of them graduated from the Zhaoge Zhuang school.

Among the Eight Great Disciples, Wang Yushan, Cui Shoushan, and Li Kunshan were known as the Three Mountains of Laiyang. They were the full inheritors of Song Zide and Jiang Hualong's praying mantis skills and their reputations were known far and wide.

Zhao Shiting and another disciple and nephew of Song Zide, Song Futing, became known as the Two Tings. Unfortunately, Song Futing was somewhat reclusive and who never had any disciples. The Three Mountains and Two Tings founded the Laiyang City Martial Arts Academy in the early 1930's. Many accomplished praying mantis masters studied and improved their skills under them.

There was also a group of disciples who graduated from the Changshan boxing school.[9] Among them, the most famous were Ji Leishan, Cui Luoting, Yuan Zi, Li Kunshan, Cao Zuohou, Liu Zuyuan, Zhao Yingting, Liu Yunde, Du Lianzhou, Liu Yuanqing, Yan Shijie, Jiang Dongyang, Yu Zhengjiang, Jia Jinting, and Yan Xuexin.

The Sixth Generation: Wang Yushan, Cui Shoushan, and Li Kunshan

Wang Yushan (1892-1976) was born in Cui Zhuang Village, Laiyang County, and was also known as Wang Zhen.[10] At the age of eight, he started learning Ground Fighting Skills boxing from his grandfather, Song Yuntong. There was a popular saying in Shandong Peninsula about Song: "In striking with essential skills, none surpassed Song Yuntong. In striking with strength, none surpassed Sun Keyang." Wang grew up to be a large man, standing five feet, eight inches and weighing 205 pounds. He diligently studied for eight years and succeeded in mastering his grandfather's boxing. He then traveled with his cousin and visited many famous martial arts experts in the area.

Wang Yushan (1892-1976).

At that time, Wang's father became friends with Jiang Hualong and Song Zide. Inquisitive young Wang visited their school, seeking a fight with Song Zide to test praying mantis boxing. At first, Wang Yushan planned to fight for ten rounds but could last only three against Song. Impressed, Wang decided to learn praying mantis. He returned home and announced to his parents and brothers that he had discovered excellent boxing techniques and that he wanted to study praying mantis boxing. His family agreed and Wang Yushan went to the boxing school of Jiang Hualong and Song Zide in Zhaoge Zhuang Village in 1910. Wang practiced twice a day for seven years. Song and Jiang would teach him in the morning and evening and Wang would practice on his own the rest of the day. He was once even expected to fight against his uncle (his mother's brother). They fought for ten rounds and Wang Yushan defeated his uncle.

Wang Yushan studied with humility and tenacity as he was taught by the two best praying mantis boxing masters. His teachers therefore allowed him to grasp the essence of their style. Wang acquired an exceptional knowledge of praying mantis practice and theory. After many years of training, Wang's skills were nearly perfect. He was 25 years old.

Wang Yushan proved himself to be an assiduous, honest, and loyal student, and therefore he was allowed to wed Master Song Zide's only daughter. According to Wang Yushan's son, Wang Yuanqian, his father had paid for his training for many years but, after the marriage, Song Zide told him that he no longer had to pay. However, Wang Yushan insisted that he continue to pay for three more years as a token of respect to his teacher.

After Wang Yushan completed his training, Master Jiang advised Wang to seek out different masters to test his fighting skills and gain experience. In old China, this practice was called "visiting friends." The next day, Wang Yushan formally left Song and Jiang's school with two other boxing brothers. Both masters accompanied them to the gates and Jiang gave the last admonition: "The hand does not wait for the hand. The ship does not wait for the passenger. Blocking the gates are punches. Blocking the gates are kicks. A powerful general should not have under his command a weak army." The meaning of this idiom can be explained as follows: whenever fighting with an expert boxer, you should attack immediately. Attack him continuously with kicks and punches so that he doesn't have an opportunity to react. Even in his late years, Wang Yushan often told this story.

In 1917, at the age of 25, Wang Yushan started teaching praying mantis and accepting disciples. Song Zide helped him establish his first school in the Laiyang area. Wang Yushan's first disciple was Wang Zijing from Beixiang Village, Laiyang County. He followed Wang Yushan for many years and his praying mantis skills became profound. Wang Zijing would later teach the founder of Secret Gates Praying Mantis Boxing, Zhang Dekui (1907-1991).

Wang Yushan's reputation preceded him on his travels. Thus people in Laiyang used to say, "The young master who arrived downtown has hands that carry far," meaning that his techniques are absolutely splendid. Many boxers challenged him. Soon after Wang opened his school, the head judge of the county court, Zhang Shenglou, who was in charge of the most hardened criminals in the county prison and who was trained in a different Chinese boxing style, decided to visit Wang Yushan's new school. He knocked at Wang's door but no one answered. When Zhang entered, nobody was there and the room was pitch dark. Wang was out having dinner. When Wang Yushan returned, he immediately sensed hostility in the air. Zhang attacked. Wang dodged and counterattacked, sending his adversary to the ground. Wang used the Hidden Dragon technique. Shaken, Zhang got up and instantly knelt in front of Wang, humbly offering his apologies. Wang accepted and said, "Stand up and tell me what you want." Zhang asked, "Master Wang, please teach me these techniques." Zhang Shenglou became a disciple and friend of Wang's. Zhang was one year older than Wang and studied assiduously, involving himself with eagerness and eventually becoming a member of the Laiyang County martial arts elite. Judge Zhang once said, "Master Wang, you should never fight one-on-one. There is no reason to do so with your exceptional boxing skills. You should only agree to fight multiple attackers; then and only then will you be truly victorious."

Another story tells us that, when Wang Yushan was twenty-eight years old, he happened to be in a village during a festival. One man was drawing water from the well by rotating a pulley. When the water basket was almost out of the well, the man's hand slipped and released the pulley handle. The heavy water basket was ready to fly down and spin the pulley handle, which would have hit the man in the head. However, Wang Yushan charged forward, throwing his iron-like arm into the spinning pulley handle, blocking it and saving the villager's life. Everybody in the village was astounded by Wang's fast reaction and great skills.

On another occasion, Wang Yushan had to buy a shotgun, so he went to Laiyang City. On the way back, he passed through Zhaixiang Village. Village official Yu Quanyong stopped him and said, "You violate the law by carrying a gun in this village, I must confiscate it." Wang answered, "I just bought it and I will register this gun when I get home." But the official did not want to listen and tried to take the weapon by force, which obliged Wang Yushan to defend himself. Yu was a very large man with great physical strength, so he said with contempt, "You are not the right size to beat me." Wang answered, "If you attack me, I will make you eat dust." Yu exclaimed, "I do not think that you know any more than those two tricky moves that you have just performed on me," and leaped like a famished wolf on Wang. Wang dodged the attack and knocked Yu down with a severe blow. An enormous crowd gathered while they were fighting. The village mayor, Yu Ziyun, brought more than thirty fellow citizens armed with sticks and ropes to seize the frightening intruder. But when the mayor recognized Wang Yushan, he hastened to declare, "This man is our kinsman Yushan of Cuitan, so stop at once." He then turned and said to Wang, "Please come and join me for dinner." Mayor Yu ordered that the best food and wine be served to Wang as he was an important guest.

The giant Yu Quanyong soon came and roared, "Who is this devil?" Mayor Yu Ziyun replied, "He is a disciple of praying mantis Master Song Zide, who teaches in Zhaoge Zhuang Village. And as you know, Yu, how could the boxing of our Zhaixiang Village compete with that of Zhaoge Zhuang Village?" Then the mayor asked Wang, "If brother Yushan has some spare time, we will be very honored if he could instruct us in his boxing."

The giant Yu spoke to Wang Yushan while staring at the floor, "Today's incident is like the history of Xiao Bayi—it is indeed in combat that a friend is discovered. Please allow me to offer you my daughter as a wife." Wang smiled and said, "I prefer to remain unmarried, but I have many nephews." Yu stumbled for a second and replied, "Well, then, I will give my daughter to one of your nephews!" Thus the story of how Wang, with a single blow, acquired a wife for his nephew quickly became known in the Laiyang area.

In the spring of 1930, Jiang Shuben of Lingshan Village, Jimo County, invited Wang Yushan to teach in Qingdao City. Once there, Wang taught at the Tenth Martial Arts Gymnasium. Jiang warned Wang about the school's bad reputation. He said that eight martial arts masters had already been beaten there and had been forced to resign. The first day, wearing a long traditional robe, Wang Yushan arrived at the school and was told that ten of the students would like to fight and test their new teacher. Wang Yushan agreed. After taking his robe off, the first four students attacked him. Soon, seven of the ten challengers were thrown, punched, or kicked to different parts of the gym and the rest refused to fight. Stunned, Jiang Shubei said, "If there are any more daring left, attack at once!" But nobody dared. Jiang Shubei and all of the students invited Wang to a welcoming dinner. In Qingdao, this incident generated a new wave of interest in Wang Yushan's praying mantis boxing.

In 1932, the Qingdao City platform fighting (*leitai*) tournament was held at the Qiyan Huiguan Boxing School. Wang Yushan went there with the disciples of Masters Liang Guocheng, Ding Shuwu and Li Pengshan. One of the few tournament rules stated that masters could fight only against other masters and students only against students. Ding and Li fought in the students division and won. Wang Yushan fought in the masters division against a man named Chi from Cangzhou. Wang first used Great Ultimate Strikes but Chi kicked him. Wang then used Pulley Strikes and threw Chi off of the platform. After the tournament, many masters came to pay their respects to Wang, praising his skills.

In the spring of 1933, the First Shandong Provincial Martial Arts Examination (Tournament)[11] was held in Jinan City. This was an eight-day event that attracted large crowds. More than 400 contestants were supposed to fight without any protective equipment or rules. When the examination reached the eighth day, Wang Yushan had defeated all challengers and was winning the last bout against a boxer who was a nephew of the Henan governor. This bout was supposed to last only three rounds. However, one of the referees, who had connections to the Henan governor, did not ring the gong at the end of the third round when he saw that the governors' nephew was losing. The second referee, Ji Yuren, who was from Qingdao, told Wang Yushan that he had to continue fighting until he knocked out the challenger; otherwise he would not recognize the victory. Wang immediately won by using the praying mantis techniques Grand Ultimate Strikes and Double-Connected Elbows, knocking his opponent out and throwing him off of the platform. The challenger was taken to the hospital, where he passed away a few days later. When Wang Yushan heard the news, he became concerned that the Henan governor would come after him. But nothing happened. After the examination, sports promoter and organizer Ma Liang (1878-1947) held a conference where he said of Wang Yushan, "When I was a referee for the First National Martial Arts Examination in 1929, every day had not run out without some serious injuries and oftentimes deaths. However, today I can say that none of the contenders of the First National Martial Arts Examination could be compared with the combat skills of praying mantis Master Wang Yushan from Laiyang City. We declare Mr. Wang Yushan victorious and let us encourage him to take part in the upcoming Second National Martial Arts Examination."

On October 20, 1933, the Second National Martial Arts Examination was held in the capital of China, which at that time was Nanjing ("Southern Capital"). As the winner of a provincial level examination, Wang Yushan was to compete in the free-fighting division. However, in comparison with the traditional and somewhat ruleless platform fighting tournaments, this event had many rules. During the First National Martial Arts Tournament, held on October 15, 1929, so many competitors were injured that, during the course of organizing this second tournament, a new set of rules geared toward the competitors' safety was developed and fully implemented. The new rules prohibited any kind of strike against an opponent's head, throat, or groin.[12]

Wang's challenger was a man from Fujian Province. This man continuously attacked by charging forward with his head down, trying to head-butt Wang. One of the hallmarks of praying mantis is attacking the head, but the new rules made most of these techniques illegal. Wang Yushan finally became frustrated with the man's fighting style and knocked the man out with a blow to the head, which disqualified Wang from the rest of the tournament.

In 1933, Wang Yushan started teaching in the recently established Laiyang Martial Arts Academy, which he co-founded with his boxing brothers Li Kunshan and Cui Shoushan. At the time, all professional martial artists of Laiyang and Yantai Counties, regardless from whom they had learned their boxing skills, were required to graduate from the Laiyang Martial Arts Academy and to obtain permission to teach on a government-sanctioned basis. Thus many Laiyang and Yantai praying mantis boxing masters learned and improved their skills in the academy, receiving instruction from the Three Mountains of Laiyang: Wang Yushan, Li Kunshan, and Cui Shoushan.

Wang Yushan was the first Grand Ultimate Praying Mantis Boxing master to teach this style in Qingdao, which he began to do in the 1930's. In the 1940's, two prominent Seven Stars Praying Mantis masters, Wang Yunpeng and Mao Liquan, taught in Qingdao. Mao Liquan became a good friend of Wang Yushan, from whom he learned some Essentials forms.

Left: Wang Yuanqian demonstrates the praying
mantis technique called "Grand Ultimate Strikes."
Right: Wang Yushan during his final fight at the Jinan tournament, 1933.

Seven Stars Praying Mantis Master Wang Yunpeng (1875-1959), a disciple of Li Zizhan (aka "Fast Hands" Li), moved to Qingdao in 1946. However, by 1951, he lost all of his disciples because of the country's difficult economic and political situation. He could not make enough money even to feed himself. At that time, Wang Yushan was treating peoples' illnesses and conditioning his students with Praying Mantis Paida qigong in one of the civil institutions of Qingdao. Wang Yunpeng, in order to make a living, got permission from Wang Yushan to learn traditional massage techniques and Paida gong from him.

One time, during a healing session in the presence of boxing masters Liu Gedan and Liu Dianxian, Wang Yunpeng declared that in Qingdao there were no martial arts masters who had beaten him and that Wang Yushan was the only one with whom he had not yet fought. Upon hearing this, Wang Yushan said, "All right, please come and attack me!" It took just a few seconds for Yushan to defeat Yunpeng. Shocked, Wang Yupeng exclaimed, "Master Wang, you are truly a real master and your skills are extremely high!" Wang Yunpeng then asked Wang Yushan to help him improve his fighting techniques. Considering their friendly relationship, Yushan taught him the first and second forms of the Grand Ultimate Praying Mantis Essentials set.

In the 1940's, Wang Yushan settled permanently in Qingdao and taught praying mantis, becoming one of the most prominent martial arts figures of the 20th century. He trained many disciples and influenced many others. Among Wang Yushan's most famous disciples were his two sons, Wang Yuanqian and Wang Yuanliang; Wang Zijing; Liu Baomin; Wang Dejun; Liu Guotang; and Zhang Shoushan. Wang Yushan won many fights against many challengers and numerous accomplished praying mantis boxing masters trained under him. Wang Yushan died on December 15, 1976.

Cui Shoushan (1890-1969), also known as Cui Pengnian, was born in Zhulu Village, Laiyang County. He started learning praying mantis in 1905 from Song Zide. In 1912, he started teaching boxing in Dalian, Liaoning Province. In 1933, he cofounded the Laiyang City Martial Arts Academy, where he taught for two years. In 1935, he was invited to Yantai by his friend, Zhang Mengjia, and his future disciple, Zhang Kaitang. There, Cui founded one of the three great boxing schools in Yantai, the Cui Shoushan Boxing School, where he taught many students and disciples. At that time, Cui obtained the *Praying Mantis Boxing Manual* written by Song Zide from his boxing brother Wang Yushan. Cui Shoushan expanded the material of the manual to two volumes, adding more general history, forms, weapons, and internal conditioning exercises. In 1937, Cui returned to Laiyang and opened the Shoushan Boxing School.

Cui's most famous disciple was Zhang Kaitang (1910-1993) from Yantai. Cui's second well-known disciple, Xu Fengqi from Xiao Xuge Zhuang Village, Laiyang County, was honored with the nickname "The Little Tiger of Laiyang." He also once held a post in the National Arts Academy of Laiyang. In the fall of 1933, the martial arts community set up a memorial stele for the prominent praying mantis boxing figure Song Zide, whom the stele described as a "Propagator of the Martial Arts" for his transmission of the style. The name of his disciple, Xu Fengqi, was also inscribed on the stele. Xu's disciple, Sun De of Dong Chengyang Cun Village in Laiyang, inherited the teachings of Grand Ultimate Praying Mantis Boxing. Sun De taught the art for many years, at times publishing articles about various techniques, theories, and strategies in Chinese martial arts magazines.

When in Yantai, Cui Shoushan also taught Sun Xiangting. One time, when Cui Shoushan's son, Cui Hongzhao, became ill, Sun Xiangting cured him. So Cui taught Sun as an expression of gratitude. Unfortunately, Sun Xiangting never passed on his knowledge to the next generation.

Cui Shoushan taught many talented and later famous disciples. Among them were Liu Zhongkai and Qu Shen, who later taught in Changchun, Heilongjiang Province.

Li Kunshan (1894-1976), also known as Jinyu, was born in Youge Zhuang Village, Laiyang County. During his childhood, Li learned Long-Range Boxing and Three Coordinations Boxing from his uncle, Li Danbai. In 1911, he became a disciple of Song Zide and Jiang Hualong and studied in Jiang

Hualong's Changshan Boxing School. In 1930, he became Huang County Police Department chief, where he became friends with renowned Six Harmonies Praying Mantis Master Ding Zicheng. In 1933, he took fourth place in broadsword at the Fifth All-China Sport Movement Competition. In the same year, he was champion in long spear sparring at the Second National Martial Arts Tournament in Nanjing. Also in 1933, he became a cofounder and president of the Laiyang Martial Arts Academy. Later, he became a martial arts consultant for the Northwest Republican Army. In 1949, Li moved to Taiwan with Jiang Jieshi's (Chiang Kai-shek) troops. In Taiwan, Li Kunshan lived in Jilong, where he opened a praying mantis school on top of a hill. While in Taiwan, he taught his son, Li Dengwu; Li Hongjie; Yu Eye; Li Chongde; Sun Hefeng; Cui Weiguo; Wang Kuiyi; Li Guoqing; and others.

The tombstone of Wang Yushan, located in the Wang family burial plot in Cui Zhuang Village.

The Seventh Generation: Wang Yuanqian

Wang Yuanqian (b. 1934) was born in Cuizhuang Village, Laiyang County, Shandong Province, to the wealthy family of renowned Grand Ultimate Praying Mantis master Wang Yushan. At an early age, Wang Yuanqian learned the authentic system as it was transmitted directly from his maternal grandfather. Wang would practice twice a day under his father's guidance and train the rest of the day on his own. It was a harsh schedule, but it was the necessity of traditional training. When Wang mastered the entire system, he accompanied his father Wang Yushan for twelve years as a teaching assistant. Wang Yuanqian officially started teaching on his own in

1970. In the early 1980's, Yuanqian participated in the National Martial Arts Survey Campaign, performing the last three sections of the Eight Elbows form, which was recorded on film. As the system's sole inheritor, Yuanqian continues to teach this style, preserving its traditional form unchanged from the times of Song Zide and Jiang Hualong.

Left to right: Cui Shoushan (1890-1969) and Li Kunshan (1894 -1976).

Left, Wang Yuanqian (b. 1934), and right demonstrating "Planting Elbow" from the "Eight Elbows" form.

Wang Yuanqian in his home village.

Left: Wang Yuanqian demonstrates a technique called
"Grinding Stone Strikes the Middle Chamber".
Right: Wang Yuanqian demonstrates "Stamping Rooster,"
one of the "Eight Stances."

General Characteristics and Practice

What does the term "Plum Blossom" mean exactly, beside the fact that it is the name of a flower on a plum tree? How does it interact with another frequently used term, Grand Ultimate (*Taiji*)? There are several definitions of these terms. In the oral tradition of Jiang Hualong's branch, as recorded in an interview with Master Wang Yuanqian:

> This style of praying mantis boxing is called Plum Blossom from when Master Jiang Hualong lived in the Yantai area and was challenged numerous times by Yantai boxing masters. His victories were repeatedly followed by people's comments, such as "Master Jiang's fighting techniques are continuous and ceaseless, and resemble petals of the plum blossom, rounded and flowing from one to another." This metaphor gradually became affiliated with this particular boxing style, constituting a new name: Plum Blossom Praying Mantis Boxing. The notion of the Grand Ultimate is reflected in the following characterization, "The picture of the Grand Ultimate is a circle of polar elements Yin and Yang interwoven into one. Praying mantis techniques embody these two polar elements of Yin and Yang, representing deceptiveness and actuality, softness and hardness. These are integrated into each other without a beginning or an end, constituting myriad transformations, as if the Grand Ultimate itself."

Although there are some straightforward moves, most praying mantis movements are fully circular, half circular, or rounded. If one carefully analyzes the trajectories of praying mantis movements, one notices that such distinctive techniques as Double-Connected Elbows, Circular Strike, Grinding Stone Hands, and Jade Ring Hands resemble the flowing motion within a circle, as uninterrupted and ceaseless as the Grand Ultimate itself. Thus the name.

Chinese philosophers and thinkers of antiquity considered the period when Earth separated from Heaven to be the Great Ultimate, the dawn and genesis of civilization, thus signifying the Grand Ultimate as the beginning of time. Consequently, this praying mantis boxing style gets its name, Grand Ultimate Praying Mantis Boxing, because of its ingenuity and authenticity as the original style.

Although there exists vast information on the general theory of Grand Ultimate Praying Mantis Boxing, this chapter only describes the "Twelve-Characters Principles," which is a verse that is supposed to be memorized and used accordingly by the style's practitioners. The "Twelve-Characters Principles" are Chinese characters (ideographs) that correspond to certain primary technical motions that define the boundaries of praying mantis techniques: contacting, sticking, linking, pressing, approaching, provoking, grabbing, moving along, moving against, lifting, grabbing, sealing, and blocking.

Traditional training in all praying mantis boxing styles except for Six Harmonies, begins with learning and perfecting the eight stances. Classical Grand Ultimate Praying Mantis Boxing teaches the following eight stances:

Mountain-climbing	*Dengshan*
Horseback-riding	*Qima*
Cold Rooster	*Hanji*
Stamping Rooster	*Taiji*
Minor	*Xiaoshi*
Twisted Sitting	*Zuopan*
Mounting-stamping	*Dengta*
Standing on One Leg	*Duli*

These were mastered for one year before the practitioner was allowed to learn any kind of forms or techniques. Then a practitioner would be trained in a single set of movements, usually practiced back and forth. These are called "numerous postures" (*lingshi*) and include:

One Step Three Punches	*Yibu Sanchui*
Five Punches	*Wuchui*
Mandarin Duck Kick	*Yuanyang Jiao*
Chopping in the Form of the Character "Ten"	*Shizi Pi*
Axe-Edge Kick and Strike with Crashing Hand	*Furen Jiao Kuangshou Da*
Small Surpassing-connecting and Mounting-collapsing	*Xiao Chaolian Dengta*

This is followed by mastering exercises called "standing postures" geared to develop specific praying mantis boxing motor skills. Eventually, the following empty-hand and weapon forms would be taught:

Crash and Fill In from Laiyang City	*Laiyang Bengbu*
Chaotically Connected	*Luanjie*
Four Sections of Eight Elbows	*Siduan Bazhou*
Seven Sections of Essentials	*Qiduan Zhaiyao*
Plum Blossom Path	*Meihua Lu*
Most Essential Hands	*Zhaiqi Yaoshou*
Great Ultimate Jade Ring Broad Sword	*Taiji Yuhuan Dao*
Great One's Purple-Golden Staff	*Taiyi Zijin Gun*
Jade Ring Double-Edged Sword	*Yuhuan Jian*
Six Harmonies Long Spear	*Liuhe Qiang*

To further strengthen the practitioner, specific body conditioning exercises such as the "Three Returns and Nine Rotations of Buddhist Arhats," "Sand Bag Punching," arm and hand toughening techniques and sparring called *lu quan* were also taught.

1-3) Author demonstrating a technique from "First Section of Essentials" empty-hand form: "Stamping Rooster."

4) Author demonstrating one of the techniques of Taiji Tanglang Quan: "Stealing Hand."

Wang Yuanqian teaching
Taiji Tanglang Quan.

Conclusion

Frequently, when people in the West refer to the praying mantis style of Chinese boxing, Seven Stars Praying Mantis Boxing comes to mind as the most popular. Grand Ultimate Praying Mantis or Plum Blossom Praying Mantis represents the oldest and most orthodox tradition of praying mantis and is the least known in the West. Its unbroken transmission goes back to the early years of the Qianlong reign (1736-1796). It was popularized throughout China by Song Zide and Jiang Hualong. During the first half of the 20th century, Grand Ultimate Praying Mantis Boxing found its way to Korea and later to Japan. This is one of the few truly realistic combat systems created in China. It lacks the flowery moves and often absurd techniques of later developments in Chinese martial arts. It preserves all of the original, undistorted techniques and classical forms as they are described in the old, handwritten manuscripts. Grand Ultimate Praying Mantis Boxing is the quintessence of combat techniques and strategies of close-range boxing.

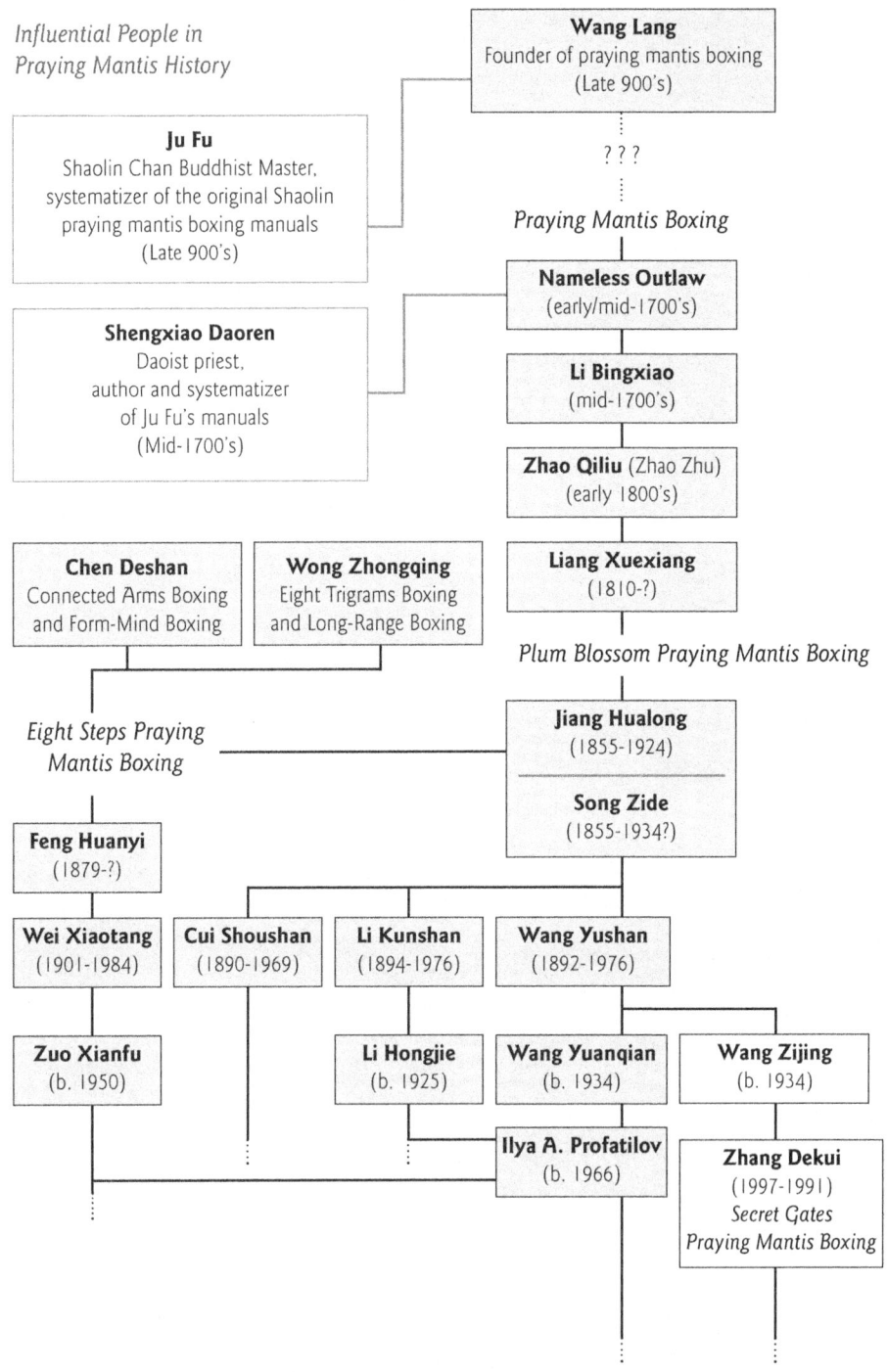

GLOSSARY

Babu Tanglauan	八步螳螂拳	Mopan Shou	磨盤手
Baguaquan	八卦拳	Qixing Tanglang Quan	七星螳螂拳
Bangzhou	幫肘	Quan Chui	圈捶
Bengbu	崩捕	Quanfang	拳房
(Laiyang Bengbu)	萊陽萊陽	Rou Tanglang	柔螳螂
Bazhou	八肘	Sanda	散打
Chang Quan	長拳	Sanhui Jiuzhuan	三迴九轉
Dadao	大盜	Luohan Gong	羅漢功
Da Shadai	打沙袋	Shi Er Zi Jue	十二字訣
Ditang	地堂	Song Zide	宋子德
Duanda	短打	Tanglang Quan	螳螂拳
Fangyou	放友	Tanglang Quanpu	螳螂拳譜
Gongfu	功夫	Taiji Da	太極打
Guoshu	國術	Taiji Meihua	太極梅花
Haojia Meihua	郝家梅花	Tanglang Quan	螳螂拳
Hou Quan	猴拳	Taiji Tanglang Quan	太極螳螂拳
Laiyang Guoshu Guan	萊陽國術館	Taiji Yuhuan Dao	太極玉環刀
Laiyang Shanshan	萊陽三山	Taiyi Zijin Gun	太乙紫金棍
Leitai	擂臺	Wang Lang	王郎
Li Bingxiao	李秉霄	Wang Yuanqian	王元乾
Li Yu Mei	力與美	Wang Yushan	王玉山
Liang Xuexiang	梁學香	Wushu	武術
Liuhe Changqiang	六合長搶	Ying Tanglang	硬螳螂
Liuhe Tanglang Quan	六合螳螂拳	Yuhuan Bu	玉環步
Liushou Fanche	六手翻車	Yuhuan Jian	玉環劍
Luanjie	亂接	Yuhuan Shou	玉環手
Meihua Lu	梅花路	Zhaiyao	摘要
Meihua Tanglang Quan	梅花螳螂拳	Zhao Zhu (Zhao Qilu)	趙珠趙起祿
Mishou	秘手	Zuoyou Di Chahua	左右底插花

Notes

1. This section is translated from Chinese Mandarin and is primarily based on tape-recorded interviews with Wang Yuanqian and on the Wang family's handwritten manuscripts. The interviews were conducted at Wang Yushan's home in Qingdao City between May 1997 and January 1999.
2. Based on this manual's stylistic writing peculiarities and its content, which are similar to the hand-copied Qing Dynasty manuscript, "Manual of Praying Mantis Boxing as Truly Transmitted Through the Teachings of the Shaolin Monastery" (1762), I believe it to be another compilation of earlier sources by Daoist priest Shengxiao Daoren.
3. Today, Da Chishan Village and Xiao Chishan Village have merged, forming Chishan Village, which is on the eastern border of Laiyang County.
4. There are no official records showing that Liang Xuexiang passed the government exams and this claim seems to be rather dubious, considering Liang's house. According to his descendant Liang Zhengzhao, Xuexiang was from a poor peasant family. It appears that he made a living by practicing traditional Chinese medicine and acupuncture before his introduction to praying mantis boxing. His fighting skills later helped him to become a bodyguard in one of Laiyang's protection and security services.
5. Li Yongde was a famous Yan Qing's Boxing master, who lived in Yantai City.
6. Three Coordinations Skills Boxing was one of two boxing styles popular in Laiyang County that emphasized ground fighting. This style was indigenous to Xixiang Village, Laiyang County; the other was from Dongxiang Village (see footnote 9). The Three Coordinations Skills curriculum included the following forms: Breaking and Grabbing, Eight Directions, Jade Ring Kicking, Continuous Five Palms, and Five Dragons Hide the Moon. Some of these forms were later incorporated into the praying mantis curriculum by Jiang Hualong and Song Zide and can be found in their hand-written praying mantis manual. Subsequently, Cui Shoushan also added Breaking and Grabbing to praying mantis boxing. Nevertheless, these forms usually are not recognized as being original praying mantis boxing forms and are taught separately.
7. The Nian Rebellion took place in north and northeast China as a counterpart to the famous anti-government Taiping Rebellion of the mid-19th century. The Nian Rebellion developed from civilian armed units called *nian* ("tied together"), which traditionally were engaged in protecting salt merchant caravans. After the end of the Opium War (1840-1842), the Nian troops' military power grew significantly. Starting around 1845, military conflicts between the Nian troops and the Qing

Government became more prevalent, which led to the beginning of the large-scale rebellion. It was finally suppressed in 1868.

8 "The Great One" is one of the numerous Daoist epithets for the Dao.

9 Ground Fighting Skills Boxing was popular in Dongxiang Village, Laiyang County, but is now extremely rare. It was transmitted by Wang Yushan's ancestor, Song Yutong, who learned it from a bandit named Deng Yude. According to the *Laiyang County Gazetteer*, "Fighting on the Ground, Long Fist, and praying mantis are the most important branches of martial arts practiced in Laiyang County. The ancestral founder of the Ditang branch was Song Yuntong. His appellation was Sida and he hailed from Shuikou Village. From his youth he excelled at the martial arts. One evening while Yuntong was at home, there came an unexpected knocking at the door in the middle of the night. The person at the door asked to see Yuntong, saying that he had come to seek asylum to avoid the consequences of some kind trouble. Yuntong took the man in and hid him behind his house, but as Yuntong was about to leave the stranger spoke again. He informed Yuntong that his name was Deng Yude. And as gratitude for Yuntong's hospitality, Deng Yude transmitted his martial arts to him. After that, Song Yutong wanderered about the south and north of the Great River [Huanghe, the Yellow River]. There he alone realized the irresistible boxing technique known as, 'A Fair Maiden Looks in the Mirror' and the saber technique called, 'Lure the Dragon Out of the Water.' Yude's disciples from the village—Song Nan, Song Tun, Wan Di, Wang Kegong, and Xu Hede, as well as Liu Ying from Jiangge Zhuang Village—were all able to pass on Yude's skills."

10 According to Wang Yushan's son, Wang Yuanqian, Deng Yude was a bandit and his original style was called "Erlang Boxing," which emphasized two-man training. Its curriculum included: the single and two-man empty-hand forms Major Throwing and Squeezing, Minor Throwing and Squeezing, Ancient Measurement Cun, A Float, Five Stepping On and Striking, Protecting the Eyes, and Stopping the Horse; and weapons forms Hitting the Hand Staff, Four Gates Whip, Four Staffs, Rubbing Staff, Lure the Dragon Out of the Water.

Cui Shoushan later incorporated the forms Major Throwing and Gripping, A Float, and Five Stepping On and Striking into the praying mantis curriculum. They can be found in volume two of his handwritten manual. Nevertheless, these forms usually are not recognized as being original praying mantis boxing forms and usually are taught separately.

11 In 1927, the traditional term "martial arts" (*wushu*) was officially changed, by the Central National Martial Arts Academy of Nanjing and under the sanction of the Nationalist Party, to "national arts" (or "national martial

arts," *guoshu*), the term used in Taiwan, Hong Kong, and Southeast Asia. The 1929 National Martial Arts Examination was based on the old imperial military examination system to determine the best in martial matters. The examination system involved a series of elimination tournaments held on village, county, provincial or city, and national levels. The National Martial Arts Examination usually was held in Nanjing. The examination system included two types of competition: "Preparatory Category," which consisted of single-man performances, empty-handed or with weapons, and "Main Category," which consisted of two-man combat bouts that were fought empty-handed or with weapons.

[12] As a result of these new rules, many famous boxing masters found themselves defeated by young, inexperienced fighters. For instance, a famous boxing master, Wang Fenglin from Tianjin, was defeated by Li Yingen, an ordinary young student of the Central National Martial Arts Academy of Nanjing. The implementation of these new non-traditional rules led to mass frustration with this event.

References
Chinese, Hand-Written Manuscripts

Cui, Shoushan. (n.d.). *Tanglang quanpu* (Praying mantis boxing manual). Laiyang, v.1, 2.

Li, Kunshan. (n.d.). *Tanglang quanpu* (Praying mantis boxing manual). Jilong.

Liang, Xuexiang. (n.d.). *Changqiang pu* (Long spear manual). Yushan Kuang.

Ma, Hanqing, and Chen, Yuntao. (n.d.). *Tanglang quan luelun* (Abridged discourse on praying mantis boxing). Beijing.

Shengxiao, Daoren. (1762). *Shaolinsi yibo zhengchuan Tanglang quanpu.* Not published.

Shengxiao, Daoren. (1794). *Tanglang quanpu* (Praying mantis boxing manual). Not published.

Song, Zide, and Jiang, Hualong. (n.d.). *Tanglang Quanpu* (Praying mantis boxing manual). Laiyang.

Publications in Chinese

Chang, Can. (1994). *Zhongguo wushu renming cidian.* Beijing: Beijing Tiyu Xueyuan Chubanshe.

De, Qian. (1988). *Shaolin wuseng zhi.* Beijing: Beijing Tiyu Xueyuan Chubanshe.

De, Qian. (1991). *Shaolin wushu daquan.* Beijing: Beijing Tiyu Xueyuan Chubanshe.

Laiyang County Gazeteer. (c. 1935). Chengwen Chubanshe. 1046-1056.

Li, Hongjie. (1992). "Yi Tang Lang quan Ming shi Li Kunshan." *Li Yu Mei*

Yekan, 28: 17.

Lin, Yongjie. (1998). *Shandong Tanglang quanshu, quanpu bian*. Hong Kong.

Ma, Xianda. (1990). *Zhongguo wushu da cidian*. Beijing.

Qi, Jiguang. Jixiao xinshu (in *Baibu zongshu jicheng*), v. 3, juan 5.

Shang, Jing, and Zhi, Bin. (1998). "Manhua Tanglang quan zhe xiang." *Wulin* 194: 52.

Wang, Kaiwen. (1996). "Tanglang quan zhi Xiangxing yu jishu tedian." *Wulin*, 1: 10.

Wang, Kaiwen, and Zhan, Yuxiang. (1998). "Meihua Tanglang quan qilu zhe shicheng." *Wuhun*, 124: 29.

Wang, Pixu. (c.1935). *Laiyang xianzhi*. Chengwen Chubanshe.

Wu, Gu, and Liu, Zhixue. (1983). *Shaolin si ziliao ji*. Beijing: Shumu Wenxian Chubanshe.

Xi, Yuntai. (1985). *Zhongguo wushu shi*. Beijing: Beijing Tiyu Xueyuan Chubanshe.

Xu, Cai. (1993). *Zhongguo wushu quanxie lu*. Beijing: Renmin Tiyu Chubanshe.

Zhang, Kongzhao. (1988). *Shaolin Zhengzong quanjing*. Beijing: Shifan Daxue Chubanshe.

Publications in English

Tao, Chengzhang. (1982). *The evolution of China's secret sects and societies* (The translation of things past, Chinese history and historiography). Hong Kong.

Interviews

Li, Hongjie. (n.d.). Interview with author.

Wang, Yuanqian. (May 1997-January 1999). Interviews with author in Qingdao, China.

Zhao, Mingde. (n.d.) Interview with author.

chapter 5

Taiji Da: A Mantis Boxing Close-Range Technique
by Ilya Profatlov, M.A.

Mantis boxing, an elegant yet highly practical branch of Chinese martial arts, has been the driving force in my life for the last twenty years. That is why I have dedicated a good part of the last decade to collecting and preserving the history and practice of the style. This extended research project has yielded a wealth of information, as well as an extended repertoire of useful combat techniques. One such technique, called *taiji da*, or grand ultimate striking, quickly became one of my favorites. Taiji da has proven to be very effective throughout history, and practicing this technique can greatly benefit any martial artist.

Five years ago, my research landed me deep in the heart of Shandong peninsula, the place where mantis boxing was first created. By this time, I had already spent a great deal of time interviewing great masters and learning their forms of Plum Blossom Mantis Boxing (*Meihua Tanglang Quan*), the oldest recorded style of mantis gongfu. Since I launched my research project in 1999, many masters had already grown old and died off, and I felt that my window of opportunity was coming to an end. After several fruitless trips to China, I was ready to give in to despondency, when a chance happening led me to visit one last village, Yuan Niu of Haiyang County. It was there that I found Lin Tangfang (林棠芳, 1920-2009), a master of Plum Blossom Mantis Boxing with skills that left me awestruck. He accepted me as a disciple and taught me his time-tested fighting system, including the invaluable principles of taiji da.

Taiji da (太極打) can best be described as a line of progression in close-range fighting. The principle of taiji da prepares the fighter to react to any number of close-range combat situations with speed and precision. Individual Plum Blossom fighting techniques can be combined in sets of three to five applications. Through the diligent practice of all Plum Blossom fighting techniques, and by applying them in logical sequences, the mantis practitioner can confidently surmount even the most menacing adversary. Nearly two hundred years ago, Liang Xuexiang (梁學香, 1810–1895) recorded in his boxing manuals a concise poem that outlines the style:

> The transformations of mantis boxing are endless,
> Mantis hands, cold rooster stance, plum blossom body, grand ultimate strikes,
> Mantis hands have tens of thousands of changes,
> In cold rooster stance, the plum blossom opens into five petals.

This poem emphasizes the importance of rigorously training basic stances and hand techniques. Once all that is up to speed, taiji da can be achieved through masterful combinations (see next pages).

Grandmaster Lin Tangfang used taiji da throughout his life to establish himself as a famous and unbeatable fighter. In his youth, Lin used these techniques to nobly protect his village from Japanese invaders during World War II. He trained the village militia in Plum Blossom Mantis techniques, and they successfully warded off the Japanese in both armed and open-hand combat. When Lin reached his late eighties, he retained every bit of his fighting spirit and ability. One day, eighty-seven-year-old Lin was out on a quiet morning walk when he was confronted by a much younger man. This man said he was looking for the infamous Lin Tangfang, in order to test his boxing skills. Lin smiled and, in order to be humble, told the man that the master had died long ago, but he was his gongfu brother. He calmly challenged the man to test his skills. The man lunged at Lin, who instantaneously met his strike with a solid taiji da. With two ironlike fingers, the old master effortlessly knocked out the man's front teeth and went on his way.

Taiji da has proven time and time again to be a highly effective principle. Through practice and determination, the use of taiji da can elevate any fighter to a new level.

The late Grandmaster Lin Tangfang (1919–2009).

Techniques: Taiji Da Combinations

When the opponent strikes (1), one must shift away from the line of attack and intercept with a double-blocking strike. The left hand acts as a soft, assisting grab, and the right hand acts as a hard block. The right hand immediately strikes the opponent in the jaw with the wrist **(2)**. If the opponent blocks **(3)**, one can pull the opponent downward **(4)**, either unbalancing him or causing him to pull back. If the opponent pulls back, one can follow and hit the opponent hard in the neck with the right straight palm **(5)**.

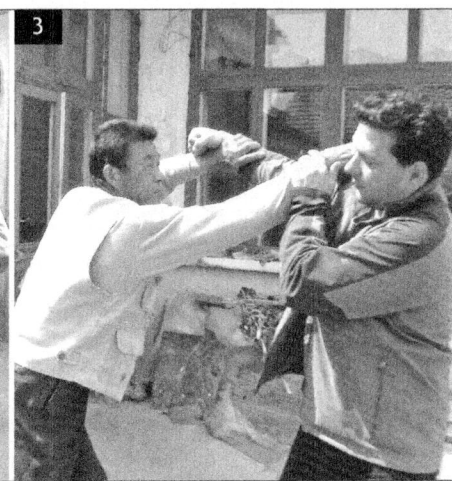

If the opponent blocks that last strike (6), one can press down on the hand and use the left "sneaking hand" to grab the opponent's wrist (7), simultaneously applying pressure on his elbow and placing the right foot on the inside of the opponent's left ankle (8). As the hands deliver the strike, one must use the right leg to deliver a solid bump to the opponent's left leg, and then sweep him diagonally to the right (9). One must take this opportunity to attack the opponent until he is immobilized (10).

index

baguazhang, 43, 53 note 2, 68
Beijing Wushu Association, 67
Boxing, Staff and Spear Fencing Manual, 63
broadsword, 68, 82
Cao, Dekun, 56
Cao, Zuohou, 74
Central National Martial Arts Academy, 92 note 11, 93 note 12
Changshan Village, 74, 82
character formula (zijue), 43-44, 51, 53 notes 1-4, and 7
Chen, Yuntao, 56
Chi, Shoujin, 56
Chin, Chuck, 11
Chishan Village, 59-60, 62, 91 note 3
classical gongfu, 2, 10
Cui, Luoting, 74
Cui, Shoushan, 56, 59, 74, 79, 81, 83, 91, 91 note 10
Daoism, 43
Ding Zichen, 82
Du, Lianzhou, 74
Eagle Claw style, 1
Eight Steps Praying Mantis, 73
Fan, Xudong, 54 note 13
Feng, Huanyi, 73
fictive kinship, 26
Fu, Ju (abbot), 57-58, 67
Funk, Jon, 54 note 12
Gong, Baotian, 68
Grand Ultimate Praying Mantis, 56, 72, 79-82, 85-86, 88
Guangxi Province's Bamboo Grove Praying Mantis, 1
Han, Tong, 57
Hao, Bin, 56
Hao, Henglu, 56

Hao, Lianru, 56, 64
hard qigong, 66, 74
Hoi Jung Temple, 1, 8
Hong Kong, 13-17, 21-26, 29-30, 35, 40-41, 44, 53 note 8, 56
Huang, Hanxun, 44, 46, 51, 53 note 8, 54 note 12
Ji, Leishan, 74
Jia, Jinting, 74
Jiang, Dongyang, 74
Jiang, Hualong, 56, 64-75, 81-83, 85, 88-89, 91 note 6
Jiang, Huanting, 68, 74
Jiang, Huanzhi, 68
Jiang, Laoqi, 64
Jiang, Yulong, 74
Jingwu Association, 53 note 8
Jiu, Zhuyuan, 74
Lee, Bao, 11
Lee, Siem, 12
Leopard style, 1
Li, Bingxiao, 58-61, 89-90
Li, Danbai, 69-71, 81
Li, Kunshan, 56, 71, 74, 79, 81-83, 89
Li, Mingge, 68
Liang, Fengzhong, 64, 66
Liang, Jingchuan, 64
Liang, Xuexiang, 61-67, 91 note 4, 89-90, 95
Liang, Zhengzhao, 64, 66, 91 note 4
Lin, Tangfang, 95-96
lion dancing, 8, 12
Liu, Yunde, 74
Liu, Yuanqing, 74
Liu, Zuyuan, 74
Long Fist (zhangquan), 92 note 9, 57, 69, 73, 81, 92 note 9
Long Spear Manual, 63-64

Lum, Wing-fai, 1, 11
Luo, Guangyu, 44, 52, 53 notes 8-9
Ma, Hanqing, 56
Mao, Liquan, 79
modern gongfu, 2
Nameless Outlaw, 58, 89
Nian Rebellion, 69, 91 note 7
Ng, Show, 11
Northern Praying Mantis Boxing, 43-44, 52, 53 note 7
Plum Blossom Praying Mantis Boxing, 55-56, 60, 84-85, 88-89, 95-96
Praying Mantis Boxing Manual, 57, 63, 67, 81
qigong, 1, 4, 12, 54 note 13, 66-67, 72, 74, 80
Qingdao city, 53 note 6, 78-80, 91 note 1
Ren, Fengrui, 56
Secret Gates Praying Mantis Boxing, 76
secret society, 14
Seven Stars Praying Mantis, 43-45, 47, 51, 53 notes 6 and 8, 54 note 12, 55-56, 79-80, 88
Shaolin Temple, 1, 43, 53 nots 6 and 13, 56-58, 67, 91 note 2
Shengxiao Daoren, 58, 67, 91 note 2
Sino-Japanese War, 2
Six Harmonies Praying Mantis Boxing, 55, 71, 73, 82, 86
Six Healing Sounds, 12
Song, Futing, 74
Song, Zide, 64, 67-68, 70-77, 81, 83, 88, 91
Southern Praying Mantis, 13, 17, 19, 23, 39
spear, 63-64, 68, 70-72, 82, 86
Su, Kebin, 56
Sun, Yuanchang, 56, 64
Sun, Ying, 64
Sun, Yuancai, 64
Sun, Yuanchang, 56, 64
sword, 2, 14, 57, 68, 71, 82, 86
Taiping Rebellion, 91 note 7
Tiger style, 1, 9
Tong, Kunjiang, 64

Yan, Shijie, 74
Yan, Xuexin, 74
Yu, Zhengjiang, 74
Yuan, Zi, 74
Yushan Kuang Village, 62-63, 66
White Crane style, 1
Wang, Guodian, 56
Wang, Lang, 44, 53 note 5, 55, 57-58, 65
Wang, Taichu, 71-72
Wang, Yongchun, 55
Wang, Yuanqian, 56, 61, 64, 67-72, 76, 80-85, 88, 91 note 1, 92 note 10
Wang, Yunpeng, 79-80
Wang, Yushan, 56, 74-82, 90, 92 note 9
Wang, Zijing, 76, 81
Wei, Xiaotang, 73
wrists, 24
wushu, 9
xingyiquan, 43, 53 note 2, 73
Xiu, Shankun, 64
Yuan Niu Village, 95
Zhang, Dekui, 76
Zang, Yunsheng, 74
Zhao, Kuangyin (emperor), 57
Zhao, Mingde, 59-61
Zhao, Qingzhi, 61
Zhao, Shiting, 74
Zhao, Yingting, 74
Zhao, Yongshou, 61
Zhao, Zhu, 56, 60-62
Zhao, Zhuxi (Chiu Chuk-kai), 56
Zhaoge Zhuang Village, 64, 72, 74-75, 77
Zhu Yongxiu, 64

Printed in Great Britain
by Amazon